Elite • 156

World War II Combat Reconnaissance Tactics

Gordon L Rottman • Illustrated by Peter Dennis
Consultant editor Martin Windrow

First published in Great Britain in 2007 by Osprey Publishing,
Midland House, West Way, Botley, Oxford OX2 0PH, UK
44-02 23rd St, Suite 219, Long Island City, NY 11101, USA
Email: info@ospreypublishing.com

Transferred to digital print on demand 2010

First published 2007
3rd impression 2008

Printed and bound in Great Britain

A CIP catalogue record for this book is available from the British Library

ISBN: 978 1 84603 137 3

Editor: Martin Windrow
Maps by The Map Studio
Page layouts by Ken Vail Graphic Design, Cambridge, UK
Typeset in Helvetica Neue and ITC New Baskerville
Index by Glyn Sutcliffe
Originated by PPS Grasmere, Leeds, UK

Artist's note

Readers may care to note that the original paintings from which the colour plates in this book were prepared are available for private sale. All reproduction copyright whatsoever is retained by the Publishers. All enquiries should be addressed to:

Peter Dennis
Fieldhead
The Park
Mansfield
Nottinghamshire
NG18 2AT
UK

The Publishers regret that they can enter into no correspondence upon this matter.

Abbreviations used in this text

AA	anti-aircraft
AFV	armoured fighting vehicle
AT	anti-tank
HQ	headquarters
I&R	intelligence and reconnaissance
LMG	light machine gun
MG	machine gun
OP	observation post
SMG	sub-machine gun

Linear measurements

Distances, ranges, and dimensions are given in inches, feet, yards, and statute miles rather than metric. To convert these figures to metric the following conversion formulas are provided:

feet to metres	multiply feet by 0.31
yards to metres	multiply yards by 0.91
miles to kilometres	multiply miles by 1.61

Title page

A German scout, with foliage stuck in his helmet band, watches for enemy movement through 6x30 binoculars. (Nik Cornish)

The Woodland Trust

Osprey Publishing is supporting the Woodland Trust, the UK's leading woodland conservation charity, by funding the dedication of trees.

www.ospreypublishing.com

Basic reconnaissance terms

English	German	Russian	Japanese
reconnaissance*	Aufklarung	razvédka	sosaku
patrol	Streife	patrul	kashikan
scout	Späher	razvédchik	sekko or teisatsu
observation post	Beobachtungsposten	nablyudéniepóst	kansokujo
outpost	Sicherungsposten	avanpóst	zensho
camouflage	Tarnung	maskiróvka	meisai

* Abbreviated 'recon' (US) and 'recce' (British)

WORLD WAR II COMBAT RECONNAISSANCE TACTICS

'NOT A STEP WITHOUT RECONNAISSANCE'

This Waffen-SS scout wears a camouflage smock in one of the many available patterns, along with a face mask made from a shelter-cape. He is adorned with vegetation to break up his silhouette and blend in with the background. His personal equipment is worn beneath the smock for additional concealment; he is armed with a 9mm MP40 machine pistol, a popular weapon to enhance patrol firepower. (Courtesy Concord Publications)

Reconnaissance is an essential aspect of warfare. It is, of course, a broad subject; this book focuses on tactical reconnaissance – i.e. at division level and below – and examines the practices employed by the United States, Great Britain, the Soviet Union, Germany and Japan. The armies of each country showed differences in unit organization, tactics and techniques, but also many similarities.

Reconnaissance tactics, techniques, unit organization and equipment were in a constant state of evolution during World War II, as the changing nature of the war brought new concepts in reconnaissance and as additional missions were assigned to these units. Specialized reconnaissance units above division level are not discussed here.[1]

The purposes and means of reconnaissance

'Reconnaissance' is the activity of reconnoitring to collect information through surveillance and examination of an area or specific site, or of enemy forces and their activities. The focus of intelligence and reconnaissance varied greatly depending on the level of command: the lower the echelon, the more detailed and precise the information had to be, and the smaller its scope and area of interest (although higher command echelons did sometimes need detailed intelligence on specifics).

At theatre level, the commander was concerned with the overall numbers of the enemy's forces, and with his capability to produce and transport materiel, weapons and equipment to the combat zone. At army group and field army levels, commanders were concerned with the enemy's long-term objectives, his abilities to shape the battlefield by shifting his forces, the number of available divisions, and the logistics to support them. The corps commander was looking at how many regiments and supporting assets the enemy could field, and what forces were available to

---

[1] See Osprey Battle Orders 12, *US Special Warfare Units in the Pacific Theater 1941–45*

Aerial photos were invaluable when maps were scarce and usually out of date. Here a pair of photos are placed side-by-side for viewing with a stereoscopic viewer; with proper focusing this would make the photo appear three-dimensional.

reinforce his defence or exploit a successful offensive. Division commanders focused on the number of battalions, artillery pieces and tanks facing them, on road networks, and the size and nature of bodies of water. A regimental/brigade commander was interested in what was on the next hill, if bridges could support his tanks, and if there were obstacles that could slow his advance.

A battalion commander was really only interested in the enemy forces he was immediately engaged with, whether the fields were too muddy for off-road movement, and how long he had before the morning fog burned off to expose his moving troops. The company commander was concerned about snipers in the woods ahead of him, if his mortars could penetrate the roofs of pillboxes, if his men could wade the streams, and if his patrols would leave tell-tale tracks through dew-covered grass.

While reconnaissance is usually imagined as carried out by patrols on the ground, it can also be conducted by examining maps and aerial photographs, by electronic interception of radio traffic, by long-range surveillance using optical devices, by aerial reconnaissance, and by observations from watercraft. Reconnaissance by ground or aircraft radar was then in its infancy, but saw some use late in World War II. Information was even collected by sound detection and ranging, especially when detecting artillery but also from the sounds made by armoured vehicles, truck traffic and other enemy activity.

Most reconnaissance was conducted covertly so that the scouts could remain undetected, avoid engagement by a superior force, and prevent the enemy knowing that they had been observed; however, there were more overt techniques. 'Reconnaissance-by-fire' was gunfire on suspected enemy positions to make him disclose his presence by returning fire or relocating. It could confirm the enemy's presence, reveal his location, and provide an estimate of his firepower, strength, and possible intentions – depending on whether he fought to retain the position, or withdrew. A 'reconnaissance-in-force' was an offensive operation intended to locate the enemy, test his strength or provoke some form of reaction.

Most commanders fully grasped the importance of reconnaissance. No matter how well led, motivated, armed, organized and supplied a force might be, thrusting blindly into enemy territory without adequate intelligence could be fatal: there were too many unknowns, and the enemy could not be relied upon to do what he had done in the past – or what it was hoped he would do. Information was needed on the identity and equipment types of enemy units; on the road network, bridges and fords, density of vegetation (as an obstacle to movement or restriction to visibility), natural and manmade obstacles and minefields; on the locations of enemy outposts, forward security forces and main line of resistance, down to the level of sub-units and heavy weapons; on reserves, assembly areas, command posts, artillery and anti-aircraft positions, supply dumps and supply routes.

The shortcomings of maps and photographs

Maps were often unavailable, inaccurate or outdated. This could partly be off-set by study of aerial photos, but these had their own limitations. The contours and obstacles beneath dense tree cover – or even thick scrub – could not be determined; nor could the elevations of even small terrain features, or the depth of flooded areas, gullies and ditches. This last was especially critical, where a difference of only inches could either halt a tank or allow it to pass. Clouds or fog could also obscure areas in aerial photographs.

The Pacific campaigns provide some examples of such problem areas. On Saipan, the US Marines discovered in aerial photos a low fold in the ground, but underestimated its height, and it halted amphibious tractors moving inland. On Peleliu the thick jungle canopy hid the exceedingly rugged hills, ridges, ravines, sinkholes and caves of the central mountains, resulting in a much longer and more costly battle than anticipated. It was common to find that the beaches of Pacific islands were backed by uncharted and impassable swamps, and for enemy-held hills and ridges to remain undetected until troops found themselves fighting their way up them. A camera could not see the underside of a bridge to determine its load capacity, or reveal whether a road or a landing beach would bear tank traffic or prove to be a quagmire.

The time factor

The entire reconnaissance process was lengthy, resource-consuming and intricate. It took time to determine what battlefield information was needed and where reconnaissance should to be focused; to allocate the assets at different echelons; to plan and co-ordinate the missions, send

What might confront a foot patrol – a scout's view of a piece of Italian terrain, with battered buildings, ravines, trees, brush and rock piles. The enemy could be anywhere, and the scout's choice of route could mean the difference between life or death.

The broken line in this manual illustration identifies the best route for a patrol. Some portions offer little concealment, but it might be sufficient if they are only under observation from a distance. Scattered, low bushes might be enough to break up a soldier's silhouette. Of course, there is always the danger of an enemy being concealed in, for example, the railroad culvert, or the woods at upper left.

them out, await their return or their reporting of information, debrief the patrols, and pass the information to the necessary headquarters (HQ); to receive, process, analyze, assess and disseminate the information, and then weave it into the operation plan.

Often that time was not available, so only part of the process could be completed – or even attempted – with unpredictable consequences. Painstaking reconnaissance might be conducted prior to specific operations such as amphibious assaults, with weeks and even months devoted to the task. Once the enemy had been engaged, however, the need to maintain a high tempo and keep up the pressure meant that little time could be allotted for detailed reconnaissance. There would, of course, be lulls in the action – when units were exhausted, or supplies could not keep pace with the attack, or contact had been lost with the enemy, or terrain or weather slowed the pace; commanders took advantage of such pauses to send out patrols to collect information and maintain or regain contact with the enemy.

Another not uncommon problem was the tendency of overly aggressive, hard-charging commanders simply not to take the time for adequate reconnaissance. There was also a reluctance by some commanders and staff to believe reconnaissance reports. This might be due to their having received bad information in the past; but they might also be reluctant to give due weight to information that did not fit their own assessment or expectations, or did not support their concept of the coming operation. If they had not 'seen it with their own eyes' they sometimes wanted the information confirmed by another source, but time and resources did not always allow this.

RECONNAISSANCE MISSIONS

Information collection and assessment

Reconnaissance units – regardless of echelon, composition, size or means of collection – have a basic mission: to gather battlefield information. They collect raw information and report it back as soon as possible – tactical battlefield information is highly perishable. The detailed pinpointing of each machine gun nest on a hill does little good if the assault troops have crossed the line of departure before the intelligence is passed down the chain-of-command.

The collector of intelligence reported what he saw, raw and unprocessed; most armies emphasized that he should make no effort to assess the information. If a scout saw ten men moving across a stream and into a clump of trees, that is what he reported – not a 'squad moving into a defensive position'. That raw information was either communicated back to headquarters, or the scout returned to his HQ and reported it during debriefing. The raw information was communicated up the chain-of-command to the headquarters echelon that had ordered the patrol. (Of course, the scout's parent unit could also make immediate use of the information based on what they knew – in this case, either level that particular clump of trees, or avoid it when advancing.)

The HQ responsible for the patrol would assess the information and then, if applicable, pass it both further up the chain-of-command and down to its own subordinate units. It might even pass it 'sideways' to adjacent units if it was of immediate use, but often it was not: patrols operated within the boundaries of their parent unit's sector, and what they discovered seldom impacted on neighbouring units. How high up the chain-of-command reports were sent depended on the level of the information; division HQ would not be interested in a handful of enemy sitting in a clump of trees, unless they had a heavy anti-tank or an anti-aircraft gun.

The assignment of missions, regardless of the tasking echelon, often fell on the rifle platoons. There was a divisional reconnaissance unit, but this worked directly for the division staff. Regiments sometimes had a platoon-size reconnaissance sub-unit; battalions usually did not. Most reconnaissance was conducted by men from infantry units, or sometimes by engineers. Not only did companies conduct their own local patrols, but their parent battalion and regiment would task the companies for missions, and these all fell on the rifle platoons who happened to be in the appropriate place.

The key task of a unit's intelligence staff was to analyze the reported information quickly (usually a rushed and rather unsophisticated procedure), to post it on maps, and to forward it to higher command levels if applicable. If of immediate importance, it might be disseminated to subordinate units by telephone or courier. It might take the form of a verbal or brief written report, a map overlay or sketch map. The intelligence section's challenge was to make speedy assessments based on experience, and to distribute the intelligence as soon as possible. The section would also receive intelligence reports and summaries from higher headquarters, and had to determine what was applicable for dissemination to their units. They also had to advise the commander and staff on known enemy activities and dispositions so that tactical plans could be developed.

Figure 4

An example of a US message form used for reporting intelligence information. Basically such patrol reports included 'who, what, when and where'.

A map overlay provided a means of transferring data without having to mark it on maps; gridline reference points were marked on the tracing paper to align it to a map, and whatever information was needed was plotted and marked on the overlay.

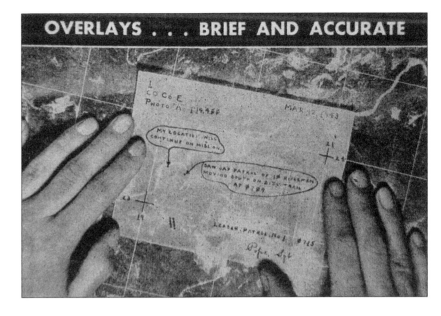

OVERLAYS . . . BRIEF AND ACCURATE

An example of a US Marine platoon ambush; black symbols = US, grey = Japanese. Counter-reconnaissance patrols became proficient at ambushing small enemy patrols.

One platoon in ambush.
Ambushing groups on both sides of trail.
Direction of enemy advance known.

WITHDRAWAL

Platoon Rally Point

Rally Point

Anti Personnel Mines

WITHDRAWAL

Reserve
one squad (less
one fire team)

one squad
(plus one
fire team)

one
squad

Rally Point

Anti Personnel Mines

Probable enemy reaction

The higher the echelon, the more time generally available for in-depth assessment. All this information from multiple units, sources, and higher HQs was analyzed and pieced together by the intelligence staff in an effort to assemble a picture of the enemy's dispositions and intent. That ten-man squad might not have been occupying a defensive position in their clump of trees; depending on the location of other identified elements and activities, it might have been occupying a security position well forward of the main line of resistance.

Inevitably, intelligence sections were sometimes wrong – or at least partly – in their assessments, and this damaged their reliability in the eyes of the commander and staff. They could only make their assessment based on available and usually incomplete information, and it was therefore, at best, an educated guess. (It has been said that there are two trades in which one is paid to make guesses: military intelligence and weather forecasting.) Due to the lack of esteem in which this work was held, it was not uncommon for intelligence officers to be selected from among the less than outstanding personnel.

Patrol tasks

The primary mission of elements conducting reconnaissance was to collect particular information; usually this was simply on the disposition and activity of enemy units – where they were and what they were doing – and on terrain and movement routes; but it might also be very specific – for example, to find a ford across a river. Engineers might be tasked with examining a bridge, or finding out if a road was mined or cratered to the point of being impassable. Patrols were, of course, always expected to report any other information of value they might discover.

A 'point reconnaissance' had the mission of scouting a specific site such as a bridge or building. Depending on the mission and tactical situation it might not be necessary for the patrol to physically visit the site, but simply to observe it from different vantage points. An 'area reconnaissance' required the patrol to reconnoitre throughout a specific area, usually searching for an enemy presence or collecting terrain information. Again, it was not always necessary for a 'route reconnaissance' to actually travel the road, rail tracks, river or other avenue for movement; the patrol might remain concealed on adjacent terrain, since its purpose was usually to determine route 'trafficability' – its condition, obstacles and enemy presence. Critical information included the surface and state of repair, any washouts or mudslides, the condition of bridges, and if ditches, walls, muddy fields or dense vegetation would prevent vehicles from pulling off it.

Patrols might be accompanied by specialists to undertake particular missions, such as checking the safety of routes of advance. Here a Red Army engineer searches for mines using a VIM-210 mine detector attached to his 7.62mm Mosin-Nagant M1891/30 rifle; the soldier behind him uses a mine probe – a steel spike fitted to a wooden pole.

Reconnaissance is often thought of simply in terms of supporting the offensive, to enhance the ability of a unit to advance against resistance; but it was also important to the defence. Patrols were necessary to determine an advancing enemy's concentration areas, preparations, and possible routes of advance; to prevent or at least hamper his patrols attempting to scout friendly positions and avenues of approach – and even to observe friendly positions from the enemy side, to confirm the effectiveness of camouflage.

While reconnaissance patrols generally made every effort to avoid detection and contact, combat patrols (in British usage, 'fighting patrols') looked for trouble. In defensive operations these included 'counter-reconnaissance' in the forms of outposts and temporary OPs to detect enemy patrols; ambushes; sniping; and roving dismounted and mounted patrols – screening missions. A small enemy patrol could be ambushed or at least driven off by fire; a larger one might not be engaged, but its location and direction could be reported, and artillery fire called down upon it if the counter-reconnaissance patrol was linked by radio or telephone – lacking these, a runner would be despatched with the information. Besides keeping enemy patrols at bay and providing early warning, such activities forced the advancing enemy to deploy from march formations into slower moving combat formations; disorganized them; and inflicted casualties and vehicle losses by direct or called-down fires.

Infantry units also established outposts to warn of enemy advances and prevent surprise attacks, sometimes augmented by regimental and divisional reconnaissance units (see Plate C). Outposts positioned to cover the most likely avenues of approach might be established by different echelon units in layers, with groups of two to four men, squads or platoons, sometimes reinforced by machine guns, AT weapons and mortars. Frontline platoons might send small teams a few hundred yards

out (usually closer), to establish outposts in daylight; at night or in poor visibility (rain, fog or snow) they placed listening posts at even shorter distances to warn of the enemy's approach. Battalions and regiments placed out-guards even further out; these might be of squad or platoon size, and their distance beyond the main line of resistance varied depending on the terrain, vegetation, visibility, and the distance of the main enemy force. These units usually came from the support (reserve) platoons and reserve companies and battalions of the infantry force.

Other missions included 'visiting patrols' to check on outposts and out-guards; 'contact patrols', to maintain contact with nearby units and to scout the areas separating them; 'connecting patrols', to maintain contact between moving elements; and 'flank patrols', to screen the flanks of moving forces. The 'commander's reconnaissance' was conducted when the commander and staff officers came forward in person to reconnoitre the terrain their unit would attack over or defend, to observe enemy positions, and simply to see for themselves the situation and conditions. They would do this from several vantage points, visiting OPs, conferring with subordinate commanders and questioning troops. This was accomplished after they had conducted a map reconnaissance and assessed whatever other information was available.

DIVISIONAL RECONNAISSANCE UNITS

Prior to World War II few armies allocated an organic reconnaissance unit to the infantry division; in wartime a battalion- or company-size cavalry unit might be attached. Reconnaissance units began to be assigned to divisions just before the war or after it commenced. (Reconnaissance units of armoured divisions were entirely different from those of infantry divisions; they were typically of battalion size, possessing large numbers of armoured cars and light tanks with considerable firepower.)

Although the size, organization, equipment, mobility and doctrine for divisional reconnaissance units varied greatly between armies, all had similar basic capabilities. These units were created to provide the division commander with a dedicated, highly mobile unit capable of collecting battlefield information, but increasingly their mobility and firepower were also exploited for combat missions.

They were routinely tasked with screening the flanks of advancing formations, or securing the exposed flanks of defending units. A frequent mission was securing those gaps between a division's units that developed through lack of enough infantry to cover a wide front. This would be accomplished by vehicle or foot patrols, observation or listening posts, squad or platoon strongpoints, or a combination of these depending on the terrain or situation. Concealed reconnaissance vehicles might be employed as mobile observation posts.

During high-tempo offensives, reconnaissance units were used for exploitation and economy-of-force missions, and might also mop up by-passed pockets of resistance. With the enemy withdrawing, disorganized and having no time to establish effective defences, reconnaissance units often provided the core of mobile task forces. They would be augmented by infantry riding on available vehicles, engineers, tanks and AT elements, to dash ahead of the slower main forces to seize key terrain and clear routes. Depending on doctrine, they might react in one of several ways when they made contact.

If encountering the enemy's out-guard, security positions, screening forces or main defensive positions, they might engage – to fix a defensive position, or drive off an out-guard or screen. Either way, if at all possible they would attempt to secure a foothold from which the main force could launch its attack into the main enemy defences. Reconnaissance troops would also secure lightly defended or undefended sites to support the

An American M8 Greyhound armoured car in Paris, 1944 – its unit identification bumper numbers have been obscured by the censor. One advantage offered by the armoured cars of divisional reconnaissance units was simply their height (here, 7ft 4in), for better observation and employment of weapons. The M8 was also used by some units of the British Army's Reconnaissance Corps allocated to infantry divisions in Italy.

FIGURE 16.—Road blocks are defended. Weapons are laid to cover routes of approach. Alternate positions are selected for vehicles.

Illustration from a US manual showing the movements of M8 armoured cars and jeeps to establish a roadblock – a key mission of most divisional reconnaissance units.

Soviet scouts armed with sub-machine guns disembark on a riverbank from an American-supplied 'seep' – the Ford GPA amphibian version of the jeep. The US Army used them in North Africa, but never took to them; they were much more popular with the Red Army, which issued them to reconnaissance units in significant numbers in 1944–45. On the Eastern Front it was more often possible to climb fairly gently sloped riverbanks than it was in NW Europe. The USSR built its own jeep-like 4∞4 GAZ-67 in modest numbers, but America shipped them thousands of Lend-Lease jeeps. (Nik Cornish)

main force's advance, such as bridges, river crossings, crossroads and dominating hills. They would also locate minefields, AT obstacles, and newly revealed impassable terrain; abandoned supply, fuel and ration dumps would be reported, along with construction materiel, water-points, and anything else useful. They might cover attached or following engineers, who would commence breaching efforts or make repairs to damaged bridges and cratered roads.

Some forces pursued less aggressive tactics. They would halt once they met resistance from anything but the lightest outposts and screens, and simply report the enemy locations, strength, weapons and obstacles. They would keep the enemy under surveillance, and harass him until the main force arrived. More aggressive reconnaissance units would do the same if resistance proved too strong. The wide variety of missions demanded that the leaders and men of reconnaissance units had to be flexible by nature, able to analyze new circumstances and adapt to them quickly.

In the defence, with enemy forward positions in close proximity, reconnaissance units could not be deployed as far out – if at all. They might be used for rear area security, especially if there was a threat of enemy airborne attack, counter-landings on beaches, infiltration or partisan activity. Reconnaissance units could also maintain contact between widely separated units, either laterally or in depth, through contact patrols. They were sometimes even used as headquarters security and honour guards, though this was generally considered a misuse of their capabilities.

Unit organization

The size of units and their designations in the different belligerent armies varied widely. Many reconnaissance units – whether horse-mounted, motorized or foot-mobile – carried cavalry lineages and traditions. In European practice, cavalry 'regiments' were actually battalion-size units comprising three or four company-size 'squadrons',

A German patrol, lacking white camouflage clothing, darts from the cover of a ravine and out across a broad snowfield. Such actions were obviously dangerous, but scouts often had no choice but to expose themselves in such a manner. They counted on the enemy not opening fire due to their desire not to reveal their positions.

each organized into 'troops' of platoon size. In US practice, a cavalry regiment had two battalion-size 'squadrons', each comprising three company-size 'troops' organized into platoons. The Soviets used a battalion/company structure for their reconnaissance units; the Japanese used battalion-size 'regiments' designated either cavalry or reconnaissance, and organized into companies. Most countries used a battalion-size unit, but the US used company-size 'troops' in the Army and 'companies' in the Marines. US armoured divisions had a reconnaissance battalion, reorganized and redesignated as an armoured cavalry squadron in 1943. Regardless of nationality, reconnaissance regiments/battalions typically had three or four squadrons/troops/companies.

These units possessed two or more means of mobility. They might have any combination of trucks, armoured and scout cars, halftracks, light tanks, tankettes, motorcycles, bicycles and horses. These varied means of mobility allowed them to operate in different kinds of terrain, and provided the flexibility to conduct different types of mission. Their weapons also varied: such units were often armed with weapons not normally found at battalion level, and other weapons, especially automatics, were issued in greater quantities. They were far from being homogenous units like most infantry and tank battalions or regiments: they were combined-arms units, with a diverse mix of weapons, mobility, and types of component sub-units, normally including a heavy element capable of delivering suppressive fire. Some sub-units had mixed equipment, with, for example, both armoured cars and scout cars or jeeps, or both bicycles and motorcycles.

The wide variety of missions assigned to these units demanded highly flexible and experienced leadership at all levels. The unit did not always operate as a single entity, and squadrons/companies were often assigned different missions scattered throughout the division's zone. Even troops/platoons could be assigned independent missions.

Either snowshoes or skis were essential for moving across country in deep snow. Here German scouts demonstrate taking cover when Russian activity is spotted; note the 'getaway man' to the rear. Besides wearing snow camouflage suits, they have whitewashed their rifles, ski poles and the upper surface of their skis.

Squadrons/companies and even platoons did not always perform these missions as 'pure' sub-units: because of their different capabilities, elements might be cross-attached between them so as to task-organize temporary specialized groups for specific missions.

All types of unit evolved during the war, but reconnaissance units did so more than many others, owing to the increase in operational tempo, the appearance of new types of vehicles and weapons, and changing concepts and assigned missions. Units of a particular army would operate and be equipped very differently from those of others, owing to the differences in operations, terrain, climate, and the enemy faced from one theatre to another. For example, a US mechanized cavalry troop in Europe operated and was equipped differently from one in the Pacific, and even a troop in the Philippines was different from one on a small South Pacific island. German reconnaissance battalions in Africa, North-West Europe and Russia were almost unrecognizable one from another.

Japanese scouts demonstrate beaching on a river bank using one-man pneumatic boats; these were provided with hand paddles and could only be used on relatively calm water, but the scouts wear kapok life vests just in case.

Regardless of what tables of organization might prescribe with regard to unit structure and equipment, more often than not units in the field varied greatly in organization, vehicles and weapons. Different vehicles were employed according to availability and restrictions of terrain and climate. Many units were more heavily armed than the standard allocation might suggest. There could even be variations between the reconnaissance units of divisions assigned to the same corps.

MOBILITY

Mobility was essential for dedicated reconnaissance units at division level; they had to cover a great deal of ground rapidly in order to get where they were needed, reconnoitre the assigned area, and return with battlefield information. Mobility became even more important when they were assigned combat missions; such economy-of-force missions required them to operate over a larger area than that assigned to normal manoeuvre units, and they also had to transport heavy weapons. It was not uncommon for them to possess organic mortars and AT guns, or at least be augmented with them. Such units relied on a wide variety of means of mobility.

Most infantry reconnaissance relied on foot mobility, owing to the need for stealth and the simple fact that virtually any terrain obstacle can be crossed by a man on foot given enough time and determination. It is a slow process, however, especially in poor visibility or harsh winter conditions, and through dense vegetation, swamps or water obstacles. Under ideal circumstances of terrain, weather and physical condition, a man can cover approximately 4 miles (6.4km) per hour on roads or good trails on level ground.[2] Hilly and mountainous terrain drastically slows the rate; in such country a realistic speed is 2½ miles (4km) per hour in daylight and 2 miles (3.2km) at night. When marching cross-country this is reduced to 1.5 miles (2.4km) per hour in daylight and 1 mile (1.6km) at night. Under tactical conditions – i.e. when attempting to avoid detection, in dense vegetation or broken ground, at night, etc. – progress may be measured in only hundreds of yards per hour; it was not uncommon for higher headquarters to have unrealistic expectations of rates of foot patrol movement until they learned from experience. Foot patrols travelled light, carrying only minimal rations, water, equipment and weapons; this allowed them to move more quickly and quietly, and conserved energy.

For infantry movement in snow conditions both skis and snowshoes might be used (see Plate G). Snow deeper than 24in (61cm) prevents foot movement; the use of snowshoes can be mastered in a few hours, but cross-country (as opposed to alpine) skiing requires several days' instruction. Snowshoes are better suited than skis to movement in dense forests, and a soldier on snowshoes can make 1½–2½ miles (2.4–4km) per hour. On skis a rate of 1½–3 miles (2.4–5.6km) per hour is possible, so that under favourable conditions a small group can cover up to 40 miles (65.3km) in a day. The Finns, Soviets and Germans made the most use of over-snow mobility. They also used small 'sled-boats' (German *Bootskaya*, Russian *volokusha*) that could be pulled by one or two men on skis or snowshoes; these were used to haul crew-served weapons, ammunition, shelter tents and stoves, and also to evacuate wounded.

Water obstacles were the most difficult to overcome. Streams, small rivers (if the main channel was not too deep) and swamps might be forded by foot troops, but large, deeper and swifter bodies of water were difficult. Swimming with equipment and weapons was virtually impossible, and left men with wet uniforms and boots, which degraded

---

[2] All movement rates suggested are based on average conditions. Actual rates can vary greatly depending on terrain, vegetation, visibility, elevation, climate, physical condition, training, morale and other factors.

Horse-mounted reconnaissance was often effective, though it had its limitations. These troops from a German regimental mounted platoon demonstrate one advantage – crossing a stream with dry boots. Dark-coloured mounts were preferred, for easier concealment; there were instances when light-coloured horses were dyed with tea or iodine solutions.

their endurance, speed and alertness. Water temperatures below 60°F (16°C) are dangerous for anything more than brief exposure, and a man then requires a dry change of uniform – which is an impractical burden for foot reconnaissance patrols. Hasty expedient flotation devices (brushwood bundles, rushes and reeds wrapped in a shelter cape, logs, etc.) were difficult to make properly, needed materials which might not be found when most needed, and still left men wet and cold.

Inflatable flotation aids and life vests might be available from engineer units, but still gave no protection from the elements. Engineer units also stocked inflatable rubber boats, small assault boats or canvas folding boats; these were heavy and bulky to carry, and were usually used only when they could be trucked to the water's edge. Such boats were propelled by paddles, which made them quiet but very slow, and they were difficult to use in strong winds and fast currents.

Horses

These were extensively used by German and Soviet reconnaissance units, and by other countries early in the war. Horses could make better time than men on foot in moderate terrain, and could wade deeper streams while keeping the rider relatively dry. In rugged terrain they could make considerably better time than foot soldiers, so long as the vegetation was moderate. Their speed was dependent on many factors of terrain, vegetation, climate and condition. While a horse can easily reach 15mph (24.1km), it can only maintain that for a short time. When covering long distances, the dismounted trooper had to walk and lead his horse for up to a quarter of the march time. Besides the rider the horse carried a considerable amount of the horse's and soldier's equipment – 25–30 per cent of their own weight. Horses suffer badly in both below-freezing weather and extremely hot climates, where they require a great deal of water; they are ill-suited for tropical and desert conditions alike. Horses have a tough time moving in unfrozen snow, and when it is frozen they have traction problems.

Horse march rates
With no limiting tactical situation or extremes of temperature, in average country on good roads, well-fed and well-conditioned horses could march at a rate of 6–6½ miles (9.6–10.4km) per hour, up to distances of about 35 miles (56km) per day. This could be extended for forced marches, but these reduced the eventual combat performance of both men and horses. In mountains, one hour was added to the time taken to cover a day's march for each 1,000ft (305m) of elevation. The US Army calculated rates of horse speed in miles per hour (1 mile = 1.6km) for each gait; the standard march gait was to alternate between walk and trot:

Walk	4mph
Trot	8mph
Canter	10mph
Manoeuvring gallop	12mph
Extended gallop	16mph

A major factor affecting the range and duration of horsed reconnaissance troops was the amount of feed and fodder that could be carried. In the field a light horse, such as employed by reconnaissance troops, required 12lb (5.4kg) of grain and 14lb (6.3kg) of hay per day: thus, 104lb (47.1kg) per horse every four days – a considerable load to carry. Wagons with feed and fodder could not keep pace with scouting troops, and had to be provided with their own security. Grazing on grass augmented but could not replace grain for stamina, and on active operations there was little time for grazing. Caring for the horse on a daily basis also required a great deal of extra time and effort on the mounted soldier's part.

Bicycles

The bicycle had been in use as a means of making infantrymen self-propelled since the latter part of the 19th century. Bicycles cost little, required few materials, were simple to operate and maintain, and were silent. Training was uncomplicated, since in an age when relatively fewer civilians had access to motor vehicles most men already knew how to ride a bike. The soldier's pack and even a light crew-served weapon could be carried on his bike rather than his back.

Good time could be made on moderate roads; an average speed of 10mph (16kph) could be maintained without undue fatigue, and 100 miles (161km) in a day was not difficult. Bicycles offered excellent mobility in areas with good roads and trails. If moving up steep hills or over difficult ground, the bike could be pushed without unloading the pack and other gear; the soldier lost nothing, even though he was temporarily on foot. When crossing streams, broken ground, gullies, dense brush or deep mud which prevented pushing it along, the bike – weighing only 50–60lb (22.7–27.2kg) – could be carried for a short distance. Bikes were of little value in mountains, swamps, dense vegetation or sand. They were useless in snow, and it was common practice to convert bicycle units to skis in the winter.[3]

---

[3] See Elite 141, *Finland at War 1939–45*

German motorcycle combinations were used to transport machine guns, 5cm mortars, ammunition, and headquarters personnel at platoon and squadron levels. The strapped bundles contain the crew's packs and bedrolls.

In North Africa and elsewhere the Germans found that light field cars were preferable to motorcycles. Most countries used four-wheel-drive vehicles, but the Wehrmacht had only the two-wheel-drive VW Kübelwagen ('tub car') SdKfz 82; this Afrika Korps example carries a 7.92mm MG34.

The American jeep
The infantry's requirement for a compact, four-wheel-drive, all-terrain utility and reconnaissance vehicle to replace the motorcycle originated in 1936, and the 'jeep' was standardized in July 1941 as the 'truck, 4∞4, ¼–ton'. Over 640,000 were built by Willys and Ford, and large numbers were supplied to the British and Commonwealth forces, Soviets and other Allied armies.
'Jeep' is said to have been a nickname for mechanics in World War I which fell from use in the 1930s. In 1936 a character was introduced in the Popeye cartoons – Eugene the Jeep – whose only words were 'Jeep, jeep'; this little creature could walk through walls, on ceilings, and go any place. Earlier vehicles called 'jeep' and believed to have been named after Eugene included ½-ton Ford trucks modified as oil exploration/survey vehicles in 1936, and the Minneapolis Moline Company's tractor-like artillery prime mover offered to the Army in 1940. It has been suggested that 'jeep' may have been derived from Ford GP – 'gee-pee' for general purpose; however, it is reported that 'GP' was actually Ford's developmental designation – 'G' for government use, 'P' the code for an 80in wheelbase. The name 'Jeep' was not trademarked until 1950. This nimble little vehicle was also known as the 'blitz wagon' or 'blitz buggy', 'bantam car' or 'peep'; the amphibian version was the 'seep'. War correspondent Ernie Pyle described the jeep as 'as faithful as a dog, as strong as a mule, and as agile as a goat'. (See Osprey New Vanguard 117, *Jeeps 1941–45*)

The Germans and Japanese made extensive and effective use of bicycles for mobile infantry and reconnaissance (see Plate F). The British used them to a limited extent within the UK; the US and Soviets basically ignored them.

Motorcycles

The solo motorcycle could carry two men and their equipment, while a motorcycle combination with a sidecar carried three; machine guns and light mortars could easily be carried. While capable of high speeds, they were noisy, and owing to their weight they had difficulty off-road or on poor trails. Their speeds were comparable to those of light cross-country trucks (below). Rough ground, mud, sand, snow, dense vegetation and steep inclines restricted their mobility; they were of little use in the Russian winter or spring and autumn mud, and in the desert their tyres quickly became shredded.

The Germans made a great deal of use of motorcycles for both reconnaissance and mobile rifle units, but by 1943 many were replaced with light trucks and other vehicles. The Soviets also fielded motorcycle units, but had the same difficulties. Most countries retained them for courier and liaison work (see Plate E).

Light trucks and cars

The concept of employing light trucks and cars for reconnaissance was not new in World War II, but the introduction of the compact four-wheel-drive cross-country truck provided a new capability. Jeep-like vehicles were small, comparatively quiet, manoeuvrable, and capable of negotiating surprisingly rough terrain, with low fuel consumption. (The US and Germany also fielded small numbers of amphibian versions.) Typically they could carry up to four men, with automatic weapons and long-range radios; their low profile made them easily concealable and a small target (see Plate D). Since they almost always lacked armour, speed was essential for survival. Top road speeds might be up to 50mph (80kph), but they normally operated at 10–25mph (16–40kph), and even slower across country and at night.

US Marines pose with a captured Nihon Nainenki 4x4 Type 95 (1935) scout car; obviously adapted from a civilian design, this was the Japanese equivalent of the jeep. Like all IJA vehicles, it was in much shorter supply than its equivalents in Allied armies. The Japanese were usually obliged to use foot, bicycle or horsed scouts, and on most Pacific islands they were almost entirely restricted to foot patrolling.

Armoured vehicles

Several types of all-wheel-drive and tracked armoured fighting vehicles (AFVs) were employed by reconnaissance units. These were comparatively light in weight, armour and armament, relying on their smaller size, speed, agility and use of natural concealment to survive. Specific characteristics varied greatly between the different types. The trend during the war was towards better armour and armament for reconnaissance AFVs, as they were increasingly used to fight for intelligence and employed for screening and economy-of-force missions.

Scout cars were small, lightly armoured four-wheel vehicles usually armed only with a machine gun, often open-topped and lacking a turret. Crews of two to four men were protected by only minimal armour against small arms fire and shell fragments.

Armoured cars were larger and heavier, with four, six or eight wheels and usually a revolving turret. Though heavier, they were still lightly armoured; they might mount multiple machine guns and/or a light cannon, usually in the 20mm–37mm range. A few types had a larger calibre gun that allowed them to place suppressive fire on enemy positions to protect other reconnaissance elements, and to fight the enemy's equivalent AFVs. All countries employed scout and armoured cars to varying degrees.

The US and Germany were the largest users of halftracks – open-topped vehicles with tracks in the rear and a pair of wheels forward for steering. They were used as command vehicles, personnel carriers, and for self-propelled heavy weapons mountings. Their armour was still light; they were less capable of negotiating rough terrain than full-tracked vehicles, and difficult to steer.

A British Daimler Dingo scout car provides an example of the lightest type of armoured fighting vehicle used by divisional reconnaissance units. They weighed 3 tons, and depended for survival upon speed (up to 55mph on roads) and agility – the original version had four-wheel steering, but this was deleted after too many inexperienced drivers rolled the car over at speed. The height of just under 5ft allowed easy concealment, but the two-man crew enjoyed only light armour protection (maximum 30mm) and firepower (one .303in Bren gun). The markings here actually identify a Free Belgian unit in 1945.

Light tanks bore somewhat heavier armour than other reconnaissance AFVs, but were still incapable of slugging it out with enemy battle tanks; they were often of obsolescent designs, relegated to this role when their value as battle tanks was overtaken by progress. They generally carried the same armament as armoured cars and had a three- or four-man crew. Their advantages were slightly better protection from enemy fire and improved cross-country mobility. A sub-category of light tanks were 'tankettes', extremely small vehicles whose concept was obsolete by World War II. Carrying a two-man crew and a machine gun, they could barely be called 'fighting vehicles', and their small size allowed only limited cross-country mobility.

Armoured cars saw widespread use by divisional reconnaissance units; they provided good cross-country mobility, the speed essential for survival, limited armour protection, and mobile firepower. The 8.7 ton, six-wheel-drive US M8 could reach 20mph cross-country and 55mph on a good road surface, and had 19mm turret and frontal armour. Its turret gun was a 37mm cannon, and it carried 80 rounds of high explosive, armour-piercing and canister ammunition. Secondary armament was a .30cal co-axial MG, and either another .30cal or a .50cal MG on a turret-top mounting.

Just as vulnerable but much more versatile and effective were the small open-topped, fully-tracked 'carriers' employed by the British and Commonwealth armies throughout the war, in numerous battlefield roles including reconnaissance (see Plate E).

WEAPONS AND EQUIPMENT

Whether infantry conducting reconnaissance or combat patrols, or mobile reconnaissance units, all such troops needed relatively light weapons offering a great deal of firepower. Foot patrols by necessity travelled light, but even if attempting to avoid contact they needed sufficient firepower to shoot their way clear if engaged by a superior enemy force. Motorized reconnaissance units also relied on firepower, since they operated far ahead of their front lines and out of range of fire support. They too had to be able to fight their way out of trouble, and needed the substantial firepower of their machine guns and light cannon to accomplish offensive economy-of-force and reconnaissance-by-fire missions.

Infantry patrols and reconnaissance units employed standard weapons, though they might carry more sub-machine guns, automatic rifles and machine guns than normally allotted to infantry. Infantry had little in the way of man-portable AT weapons before mid 1943 and were pretty much limited to AT hand and rifle grenades, overly heavy and mostly ineffective AT rifles, and expedient weapons of limited value. In some instances light AT guns were employed, but since these required motor transport they were impractical for many missions; they might be used by static out-guards, or to cover patrols as they moved forward. In 1943 weapons capable of being carried and operated by one or two men began to appear, e.g. the US bazooka, British PIAT, and German *Panzerfaust* and *Panzerschreck*. The Soviets continued to rely on 14.5mm AT rifles and AT hand grenades, while the Japanese used mainly hand-delivered AT demolitions and grenades.[4]

Light mortars in the 50/60mm range were sometimes used by combat patrols, but ammunition supply was limited if foot-mobile. Their range was usually less than 1,000 yards, but since they normally engaged only at relatively close-range, line-of-sight targets anything more was unnecessary. If linked to headquarters by radio or field telephone, patrols could call for heavier mortar and field artillery support.

Equipment

As with weapons, reconnaissance units mostly used standard equipment, but to navigate to the objective a compass is essential. A compass does more than just indicate north and provide an azimuth (direction) to follow: in conjunction with a map, it can be used to determine the location of an unknown point or a patrol's location by 'intersection' and 'resection' (see Plate A).

Binoculars are necessary for detecting and observing enemy activity and examining terrain for its nature and signs of the enemy. They are also useful at night to some degree, providing the ability to look 'into' shadows. Typical binoculars were of 6x or 7x power. Most had statia lines on the lens, allowing the range and width of targets to be estimated. Other optical instruments used included hand-held periscopes, observation telescopes, and small coincidence rangefinders.

Maps were obviously necessary for navigation and plotting battlefield information. 'Friendly' data was not supposed to be marked on maps for security reasons, but information on the enemy could be. Rather than marking information and updates directly on maps, they could be written on tracing-paper overlays. Military maps were overprinted with grid systems (normally 1,000-yard/metre squares) to allow the precise plotting of locations and the designation of points; such systems often differed between countries. Maps were usually outdated, and reconnaissance units were expected to record changes to be reported to higher headquarters. If insufficient maps were available patrols were provided with simple sketch maps with key landmarks indicated. Aerial photos were sometimes used as more up-to-date alternatives to maps.

For night patrols a flashlight (torch) was necessary for reading a map, shielded by a shelter cape, and was sometimes used for signalling. A watch was carried to record the times observations were made, to maintain time schedules and make radio reports at pre-agreed times.

---

[4] See Elite 124, *World War II Infantry Anti-Tank Tactics*

A British patrol moves briskly across an open space in a wrecked Italian town abandoned by the Germans. Such patrols became routine as the Allies pursued the withdrawing enemy, and it took concentration not to relax security. These soldiers have dumped their web equipment but have plenty of firepower: the patrol leader, with a Thompson SMG, is followed by a rifleman, another Tommy-gunner, and an LMG team with a Bren and a rifle.

In all armies the rifle squad (British, section; German, Gruppe) provided the basis of infantry patrols; here a German squad pose for a comrade's camera. Apart from the kneeling Unteroffizier squad leader, all wear their Zeltbahn camouflage shelter-capes – besides rain protection and ground camouflage, these offered concealment from enemy aircraft. Many patrols operated lightly armed, but the German squad habitually carried their 7.92mm MG34 machine gun with them. (Courtesy Concord Publications)

Clothing

Standard seasonal field uniforms were the norm for infantry reconnaissance units; camouflage uniforms were occasionally issued, but these were seldom specific to reconnaissance troops. The US Army and Marines made some use of reversible camouflage uniforms in the Pacific in 1943/44, but these soon fell out of use, since the fabric was too heavy and the design was poor. In 1944–45 British infantry scout/snipers made limited use of the airborne troops' Denison camouflage smock, when they could get hold of it. In the last months of the war the camouflaged version of the windproof smock and overtrousers originally developed for British mountain troops was quite widely issued to infantry units in Europe, though not specifically for reconnaissance use. The Soviets did issue one-piece camouflage-printed suits to some reconnaissance troops and snipers.[5]

The Japanese, while masters of expedient camouflage, did not issue uniforms printed with camouflage patterns, though caped jerkins made from vegetable fibres were quite widely made up in the field (see Plate H). The German Army only received fairly minimal issues of camouflage-printed smocks late in the war; as in the British Army, such garments were not routinely available to the riflemen who carried out most infantry patrols. The Waffen-SS used camouflage-printed uniforms the most widely, these being general issue to infantry and some other units.

Many nationalities, including the Soviets and Japanese, sometimes used small individual camouflage nets garnished with foliage. Helmets in particular were camouflaged to break up their distinctive silhouette and prevent reflections; some armies issued helmet bands and nets to hold vegetation, and helmets themselves were painted in dull camouflage patterns. Printed camouflage helmet covers were issued to the US Marine Corps, the Waffen-SS, some Luftwaffe paratroopers, and in much more limited numbers to the German Army.

[5] See Elite 68, *The Military Sniper since 1914*

US Marines cross a knee-deep stream; constant wetness was a fact of life in the jungle. Camouflage uniforms and helmet covers were effective in such terrain, but the US issue uniform was too hot and heavy, and was soon discarded in favour of olive drab utilities in herringbone twill. In Normandy the US Army withdrew limited issues of camouflage-printed uniforms after they were mistaken for Waffen-SS combat clothing.

White snow camouflage suits were issued to the US Army, more widely to British infantry, and most widely of all to Finnish, Soviet, and later to German troops (see Plate G). From 1943 the German Army and Waffen-SS received padded winter uniforms reversible from printed camouflage patterns to plain white.

Communications

Prior to World War II reconnaissance units relied mostly on couriers – foot, mounted or motorized – to report intelligence information. The other means that were tried, including field telephones and telegraph, signal and semaphore flags, signal lights, heliographs, bugles and carrier pigeons – all had obvious limitations, but were still employed early in World War II. The portable radio transmitter/receiver was a major breakthrough in the conduct of all military operations, and had a significant effect on intelligence reporting. Information could now be reported in near real-time, and contributed greatly to the speed of operations that characterized World War II.

Radio or 'wireless' had been used to a limited extent in World War I, but radio theory was not fully understood and development was a great deal slower than in other fields of technology. During the interwar years radios were improved to the point that they were light and strong enough to be transported by soldiers or carried in vehicles, and many refinements were made in their operation; however, they still had serious limitations. While some were man-portable they were still heavy, and some had to be broken down into two or more pack loads with the receiver and transmitter carried separately, along with batteries or a hand-cranked power generator, antenna and accessories. They were temperamental, required precise frequency tuning and calibration, and still demanded gentle handling due to their soldered connections and fragile vacuum tubes.

There were two types of radio. Most were amplitude modulated (AM); these achieved long range, but used continuous wave (CW) transmission,

RIGHT **Period radios were heavy, fragile and temperamental, and long-range sets were only practical for reconnaissance troops equipped with vehicles. Here German scouts in snow suits hitch a ride to their departure point on a StuG III assault gun; their backpack Torn.fu.1 (Tornisterfunkgerät) radio could not normally be operated on the move, but here it is set up on top of the armoured vehicle. (Courtesy Concord Publications)**

BELOW **The US Army's SCR-511 was the principal small sub-unit radio until 1943, when the SCR-536 'handie-talkie' was introduced. This manual illustration demonstrates the complexity of the small, short-range sets of the 1940s. The SCR-511, with a range of only a couple of miles, was originally developed for horsed cavalry, to provide mounted reconnaissance patrols with a rapid means of reporting information. The staff on the bottom of the set allowed it to be slotted into a guidon-carrier on a horseman's stirrup.**

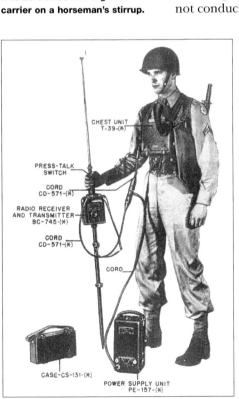

CHEST UNIT T-39-(*)

PRESS-TALK SWITCH

CORD CD-571-(*)

RADIO RECEIVER AND TRANSMITTER BC-745-(*)

CORD CD-571-(*)

CORD

CASE-CS-131-(*)

POWER SUPPLY UNIT PE-157-(*)

most often by manual code (Morse code). They could not be operated on the move, but had to be set up with a long wire antenna strung in a certain direction; the message had to be transmitted while the radio was powered by a hand-cranked generator continuously recharging the heavy battery – a time-consuming process, and hard to conceal. They could transmit voice messages, but only to much shorter ranges; reception was unreliable due to atmospheric interference or static from other stations. AM radios were not conducive to fast-moving situations.

Frequency modulated (FM) radios came into wider use as the war progressed. These were lighter, more compact sets that could be man-packed in a single unit, or even hand-held. However, FM radios were capable only of line-of-sight communication – this does not mean that the sending and receiving operators had to be able to see one another, but that mountains or high ridges between them would block signals. Contrary to what is depicted in movies, these radios had very short ranges; the American 'handie-talkie' had a range of only about a mile, and the back-packed 'walkie-talkie' 3–5 miles. They relied on batteries, which were heavy to carry and were expended at a high rate. Their frequency coverage was limited, and often radios of one type could not net with another type.

Vehicle-mounted radios might have a longer range, though not by much, unless they were AM CW; but they did have the advantage of being powered off the vehicle's electrical system. Motorized reconnaissance units were usually well equipped with radios, often possessing more than even tank units.

Field telephones were more widely used for reconnaissance than is realized. Static observation posts (OPs), listening posts and out-guard positions would be linked to their higher headquarters by land-line. Neither was it uncommon for patrols travelling only a few hundred yards to trail field wire behind them, so as to be able to report immediately and call down fire. There were limitations, but since few armies had enough man-portable radios to provide them for all patrols it was better than nothing.

Other means were used to mark patrol positions, especially to friendly aircraft – an essential requirement, since they were operating forward of the front line and aircraft did not have direct radio contact with ground forces. Coloured marker panels and in some cases national flags were laid flat on the ground or fastened atop vehicles. This was especially critical for motorized reconnaissance units, as prowling aircraft were notoriously unselective about what vehicles they attacked. Coloured panels were also used to convey simple messages, spelling out letters or geometric symbols. The US used red, yellow, black and white panels to configure code letters or symbols with pre-planned meanings. The Japanese used a complex system of long white panels laid out in a T-shape to mark the flanks and centre of positions; narrower red, black or blue panels were laid on the white so that they would appear as white-edged, and small white triangular panels were positioned in particular ways in relation to the 'T' to indicate the specific unit down to battalion level. (For example, a divisional reconnaissance regiment had blue panels laid atop the white, with a triangle on the bottom end of the 'T' and another angled off the right end of the crossbar). This system was clearly devised behind a desk somewhere, and its actual utility under battle conditions seems questionable.

Coloured smoke grenades, smoke candles, or pyrotechnic projectiles fired from signal pistols or rifle grenade launchers were used to mark friendly and enemy positions and to convey simple messages (see Plate F). Caution was obviously necessary, as the enemy would sometimes attempt to use their own coloured smoke and flares to mislead or confuse friendly aircraft. Flares in particular colours or combinations might signal a situation, e.g., 'have been engaged by enemy' or 'friendly patrol returning'; an order to initiate some action – 'lift or shift fires', 'repeat last fire mission', 'withdraw or disengage', 'cease fire'; or a report, e.g. 'objective secured'.

Patrol internal communications were by whispered commands, arm and hand signals, and – once engaged – sometimes by whistles. Motorized reconnaissance units sometimes used pairs of hand-held coloured flags to convey orders, movement directions and formation changes.

TACTICS AND TECHNIQUES

Composition of patrols
Regardless of nationality, reconnaissance patrols conducted by infantry units were similar. There were few national differences in organization between infantry sub-units, and patrols were the work of the platoon and squad. ('Squad', the US

The Torn.fu.1 backpack radio equipment was the main type used at German company and battalion levels. One of the two cases held the transmitter and receiver, and the other the power supply and accessories, which included the disassembled antennae; this radio could only be operated when set up with pole or wire antennae. This limited its usefulness to reconnaissance patrols. (Courtesy Concord Publications)

25

An American patrol prepares to set out on its mission. Helmets were sometimes left behind to reduce weight, to improve hearing and vision, and to avoid noise and a distinctive silhouette. Note that their equipment is light, with most carrying only a single bandolier of ammunition – reconnaissance patrols only carried enough to enable them to break contact.

term, is used generically in this text, to cover e.g. the British and Commonwealth 'section' and the German 'Gruppe'). A rifle platoon had a small headquarters led by a lieutenant (or senior NCO) and a platoon sergeant, sometimes with some light crew-served weapons; and three (in the German and Soviet forces, sometimes four) rifle squads. A squad consisted of eight to 14 men led by a corporal or sergeant, with one or two light machine guns or automatic rifles, and at least one rifle grenade launcher. Apart from machine-gunners most men were armed with rifles, although one or more sub-machine guns might be available; hand grenades and bayonets backed the shoulder weapons. From 1943 light portable AT weapons began to be issued to platoons, and sometimes to squads.

The basic patrol sub-unit was the rifle squad. Most squads operated as a rifle group led by the squad leader, and a two-to-four-man automatic weapon group, sometimes led by the assistant squad leader and carrying one automatic rifle (AR) or light machine gun (LMG).[6] Manning and assignments changed somewhat during the war, but typically the 12-man US Army squad had a leader, assistant leader, two-man AR team and eight riflemen. In April 1944 the US Marines changed from this organization to a 13-man squad with a leader, and three fireteams each with a leader, a two-man AR team and one rifleman. The ten-man British and Commonwealth section differed from the US Army in having six riflemen, and the 13-man Japanese section, nine riflemen. The Red Army platoon usually had two nine-man sections each with five riflemen and one LMG, and one nine-man section with three riflemen and two LMGs; early in the war 11-man sections had the same imbalance.

In combat it was not uncommon for squads to number only five to seven men. In most squads one rifleman was designated as an ammunition carrier for the AR/LMG, and one rifleman sometimes carried a rifle grenade launcher. British, Soviet and German squad leaders usually had a sub-machine gun. (Note that specialized squads

[6] See also Elite 105, *World War II Infantry Tactics: Squad and Platoon*

such as those in airborne, motorized/armoured infantry, commando/ranger/raider units and others were organized somewhat differently.)

Patrols were built around squads and platoons, augmented or reduced in size as necessary. Standard weapons might be reinforced by additional firepower depending upon mission, terrain and enemy situation. Demolition materials might be carried by combat patrols to destroy enemy equipment or defeat fortifications.

Although there were norms of organization, careful consideration was given to the size of a patrol. The smaller the patrol the better chance it had of remaining undetected – it made less noise and broke a less noticeable trail. Small patrols were also easier to control in rough terrain and poor visibility, and made faster time. However, even if infiltrating or operating close to enemy lines simply to collect information, the chance of contact was high and patrols needed to be well armed. If engaged, small patrols had less chance of surviving, so a balance of these factors had to be sought: for instance, issuing extra automatic weapons to, say, a six-man patrol would not give it a much better chance if it ran into an enemy platoon than if it were just armed with rifles.

For some reconnaissance and short-range local security patrols, often only three or four men were sent out without a squad automatic weapon. Their job was simply to report what they saw and avoid contact; typically, one man would trail to the rear – the 'getaway man', who might escape to bring back word if they were ambushed.

Where enemy contact was likely a squad-size patrol had the benefits not only of firepower but of accustomed leadership, cohesion and mutual familiarity. A patrol with a combat mission might be tasked with ambushing or driving off enemy patrols, or snatching a prisoner; of harassing or probing enemy forward positions; of infiltrating into enemy lines to attack facilities in the rear; or of attacking a specific frontline target – a raid. For such missions the rifle squad might be reinforced with part of another or even a second full squad; in such cases the patrol might be led by the platoon commander, platoon sergeant, or simply the senior squad leader.

A full platoon, possibly reinforced with extra crew-served weapons, might be assigned for certain combat missions, but patrols of this size were infrequent. A platoon might set out and, once in the area to be reconnoitred, break up into smaller patrols each assigned a specific point, area or route. Besides crew-served weapons, a patrol might occasionally have attached specialist personnel such as engineers, a demolitions man, photographer, interpreter or local guide.

The patrol leader always designated an assistant, who normally brought up the rear to ensure that no one got

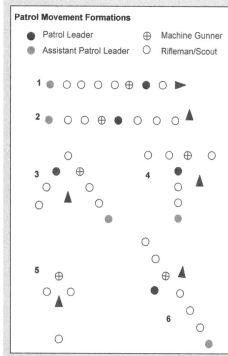

Patrol Movement Formations

● Patrol Leader   ⊕ Machine Gunner
● Assistant Patrol Leader   ○ Rifleman/Scout

Patrol movement formations vary depending on the tactical situation, terrain and visibility. These examples mostly depict an eight-man patrol. The positions of the leader, his assistant, and the machine-gunner might change depending on the situation, for different control requirements, or even at personal preference; intervals between individuals also varied.

(1) Single file was used in dense vegetation and poor visibility where ease of control and speed were necessary; on open terrain the column might be staggered.

(2) The skirmish line was used to sweep an area or when contact was expected to the front.

(3) The wedge or arrowhead offered observation and fire to the front and flanks simultaneously; but it was slow and difficult to control, especially on broken or overgrown terrain or in poor visibility.

(4) The 'T' was little used, but offered observation and fire to the front and flanks; if it was engaged from the front, the tail would swing right or left to come up into line.

(5) A small reconnaissance patrol used this type of formation, with a 'getaway man' trailing within sight.

(6) The echelon (here 'echelon right') was also slow and difficult to control, but was useful in some situations.

German NCOs prepare to take a patrol out; both carry 6x30 universal binoculars, and the Oberfeldwebel (right) has a report/map case for carrying maps, terrain sketches, overlays and report forms. The Unteroffizier (left) is armed with a Soviet 7.62mm PPSh-41 sub-machine gun with 70-round drum magazine – not because it was preferred to the MP40, but simply to augment the patrol's automatic firepower.

Patrol inspection
Prior to departing on a patrol the patrol leader inspected his men to ensure that they were prepared, capable, and had everything necessary to complete the mission.
He checked specifically that:

- Each man was physically fit for the duty, and had the prescribed uniform and equipment, adequate for the weather.
- Each man's weapon was clean and operational, with the required ammunition supply; that his canteen was full, and he had the required rations.
- No unnecessary equipment was being carried, nor any insignia, documents, letters, etc. that could identify the unit; and that nothing reflected light or rattled.
- Each man knew the challenge and password, his duties and his place in the formation, and understood the patrol's mission.
- Any radio was operational and provided with the necessary batteries, frequencies, callsigns and codes.
- A flashlight (torch) was carried for a night patrol.

separated – an easy thing to happen in broken ground and poor visibility. For large patrols subordinate leaders would be designated, not just to lead squads but for specific tasks: for example, if the objective to be reconnoitred was large, two or more two-man reconnaissance teams might approach it from different points and a leader would be designated for each. Subordinate leaders might be designated for a prisoner snatch team, rear or flank security elements for a raid, a search team to recover documents and other items in an ambush, a demolition team, fire and assault teams during a raid, and so forth. Alternates were designated for key leaders.

The patrol leader placed himself just to the rear of the lead men or man, and usually navigated with map and compass. Another man might be designated to keep the pace count if moving at night, to help estimate the distance travelled. Each man was assigned a sector of observation and fire for when moving, halted or engaged. The squad automatic weapon/s might be ahead of or immediately behind the patrol leader, for the sake of control, but it would always be well forward in the formation to allow it to get into action rapidly, whether to the front or a flank. Other crew-served weapons were positioned at intervals.

NATIONAL COMPARISONS

UNITED STATES
The long American tradition of scouting, dating from before the Revolutionary War and through the Civil War and Indian Wars, had implanted the importance of reconnaissance in the military mind. Cavalry was the standard-bearer of reconnaissance in the US Army, owing to the long distances involved. The Marine Corps was mostly concerned with beach reconnaissance, but placed importance on tactical scouting.

US Cavalry Reconnaissance Troop, Mechanized
.30cal rifles x 31, .30cal carbines x 129, .45cal SMGs x 26; .30cal MGs x 25, .50cal MGs x 16, 60mm mortars x 9, 2.36in bazookas x 5
Armoured cars x 13; halftracks x 4; trucks x 2; jeeps x 24
Personnel x 155.

Regardless of these traditions, Army and Marine divisions possessed only a company-size reconnaissance unit instead of the battalion-size units found in most armies. A 155-man *mechanized reconnaissance troop* was assigned to the new triangular infantry division in September 1940, equipped with MG-armed open-topped White M3A1 scout cars and jeeps. In July 1943 this element was redesignated a *cavalry reconnaissance troop*. In most instances they bore the number of their parent division, e.g. 7th Cavalry Reconnaissance Troop assigned to the 7th Infantry Division.

After studying British and German reconnaissance operations, the Tank Destroyer Command requested an armoured car, and this resulted in the 37mm-armed M8 Greyhound (the similar M20 armoured utility car, with an open-topped compartment and a .50cal MG, was not used by reconnaissance troops, only by TD units). The M8 was not fielded until mid-1943; in the meantime M3A1 scout cars, one in each section of three towing a 37mm AT gun, were used; M3A1 halftracks were also employed as substitutes, and some units retained these into 1944.

The troop had a headquarters, with three M8s and four jeeps in the headquarters section, plus administration, supply and mess elements which together had an M8, four halftracks, two 2½-ton trucks and two jeeps. The three reconnaissance platoons were each divided into an

This annotated aerial photo illustrates a platoon-size US combat patrol conducted in mountainous Italian terrain, and suggests the intricate planning involved. The details are not clearly visible here, but the original tells a complex story. Enemy positions and lines are shown (dark blocks on castellated lines, with radiating arrows for their fields of fire).

The patrol left US lines (slanting castellated line at bottom left) at the initial point (IP), and moved up the photo – its route indicated by a solid arrowed line – while keeping below a ridge line to avoid being silhouetted, to Checkpoint 1 (CP 1). From there it followed a ravine east and then north to the base of a ridge finger. There one rifle squad, reinforced with a machine gun, separated, and moved north up an eastern ridge finger (broken arrowed line); they would provide supporting fire for the assault on the objective – (O). The attack element moved north up the western ridge finger, pausing at CP 2 to confirm their progress to HQ; they then moved to the objective, raided the position and captured a prisoner. Withdrawing south-westwards to CP 3, they reported their success and estimated their arrival time in US lines, which they crossed slightly west of the IP. The support element probably retraced their outbound route back to the IP, or could have moved laterally through ravines north of CP 1 to link up with the main body at CP 3.

An American patrol crosses a stream on one of the larger Pacific islands. This demonstrates the density of jungle vegetation, which offered excellent concealment to scouts – but also to enemy counter-reconnaissance patrols, resulting in sudden close-range firefights. Dense vegetation also greatly slowed patrol movement rates.

armoured car section with three M8s or halftracks, and a scout section with three .30cal MG-armed jeeps and three more carrying 60mm mortars – these operated in three pairs as squads.

In the Pacific Theatre the troops tended to be lighter; vehicles varied, but on Pacific islands they often operated on foot or used jeeps. In the larger Philippine islands, with their better road networks, they normally operated with armoured cars.

Airborne divisions lacked a reconnaissance unit, but formed provisional jeep-mounted 32-man recon platoons; this was formalized in late 1944/early 1945. The platoon could jump in and operate on foot until their jeeps were delivered later by glider, transport aircraft or the sea-borne echelon. Armoured divisions had a *reconnaissance battalion (armored)*, redesignated a *cavalry reconnaissance squadron, mechanized* in September 1943.

From 1941 the Marine division was assigned a 175-man *scout company* organic to the light tank battalion and designated, e.g., Co E (Scout), 1st Light Tank Battalion in the 1st Marine Division. Assigned to the tank battalion in order to share maintenance facilities, they originally had three scout car platoons each with four M3A1s, and a scout platoon with four jeeps and four motorcycles. In late 1942, before any saw action, they were reorganized into four platoons each with eight jeeps, the scout cars and motorcycles being unsuited for tropical islands. Even the jeeps were found unnecessary, and the scouts operated on foot or used rubber boats. No longer requiring vehicle maintenance support, the now 139-man companies were removed from the tank battalions in the summer/fall of 1943 and reassigned to the division headquarters battalion as, e.g., Scout Co, Headquarter Bn, 1st Marine Division. In spring 1944 they were assigned numbers matching their parent division and redesignated, e.g., 1st Reconnaissance Company. They now consisted of three small foot/boat-mobile platoons totalling 127 men and not a single vehicle.

These companies performed some common tasks and others unique to Pacific island fighting. They secured gaps between regiments, especially when the terrain was extremely rough; acted as a divisional reserve, as a reserve or reinforcement for a depleted regiment; provided beach defence to protect against Japanese counter-landings, for rear area mop-up, a second defence line to halt infiltrators, and headquarters security. They were also assigned offensive missions, being landed on atoll islets to clear Japanese lookouts or stragglers, and in some cases to secure islets adjacent to a larger objective island from which artillery battalions would support the main landing.[7]

The Army infantry regiment was assigned an *intelligence and reconnaissance (I&R) platoon* in the HQ company. This 25-man platoon had a headquarters with one jeep mounting a .50cal MG, and two three-jeep squads – supposedly unarmed, but in practice at least some mounting .30cal or .50cal guns. The infantry battalion had an intelligence sergeant and six intelligence scout/observers; these could assist the intelligence officer in the command post, or would sometimes help man OPs or accompany patrols as collection specialists. There were instances when battalions formed their own I&R sections or platoons, using the intelligence scouts as a cadre augmented with volunteers; these might have vehicles or operate dismounted. Parachute and glider infantry regiments lacked an I&R platoon, but sometimes the demolition platoon would be employed as scouts.

Marine regimental and battalion headquarters had similar intelligence scouts to accompany patrols. In April 1943 a 33-man scout/sniper platoon was added to the regimental HQ&S company; while this was of value, there was more need for assault troops, and the platoon was deleted in April 1944.

Army and Marine rifle squads initially had two men designated as scouts. The concept was for the squad leader and scouts to move in advance of the rest of the squad and the assistant squad leader; this proved impractical, since they would often become early casualties or get pinned down. The practice, soon scrapped, was formally dropped in 1944, and the scouts became riflemen – for all practical purposes, all riflemen were scouts.

* * *

As described above, infantry patrols were usually conducted by rifle squads, sometimes reinforced; on Pacific islands, where dense vegetation greatly limited visibility, larger patrols were the rule – if engaged, they needed the firepower to fight their way out. Generally reconnaissance patrols as large as a platoon were rare, and there were instances when two- and three-man patrols were used. Rifle platoons only had a single 'handie-talkie' radio with a one-mile range, and these were not widely available until late 1943; in the jungle, short range patrols maintained contact with field telephones, trailing the wire behind, but elsewhere this was often impractical.

Regardless of terrain, reconnaissance patrols were taught to advance in bounds from one concealing terrain feature to the next. When they got close to the enemy the bounds were shorter, and when

The elevation provided by armoured cars improved observation and weapons employment, but a high profile also made them easier to detect and hit. This drawback is demonstrated by a British Humber Mk II armoured car (about 7ft 8in tall) of an infantry division's integral battalion-size regiment of the Reconnaissance Corps. The Mk II had a crew of three, and 15mm and 7.92mm Besa turret machine guns; the later Mk IV had the same 37mm gun as the US Greyhound. The Humber weighed 6.4 tons loaded, and had a top road speed of 45mph.

approaching a suspected position a single scout was sent ahead, covered by the rest of the patrol – if it was clear, he waved the patrol forward. Usually men were taught to work in pairs. The 'getaway man' concept was practiced, especially in small patrols. Patrols maintained a dispersed formation depending on the terrain, vegetation and visibility. Each man was assigned a sector of observation, when both moving and halted (rest halts were brief, to reduce the risk of detection). In dense vegetation patrols typically assumed single file, but in less thick cover they opened out into a dispersed formation. A scout might precede the patrol by up to 150 yards, but in actual combat this was seldom done due to the high risk of his becoming separated or being spotted. When reconnoitring a specific area patrols would form a skirmish line to cover as much ground as possible. Particular care was taken when crossing danger areas – roads, streams, fences, clearings and other points of exposure.

Patrol plans were often intricate, as suggested by the accompanying annotated aerial photo on page 29. A common criticism of American patrols made by the Germans and Japanese was that they lacked patience – that they were too impetuous to remain motionless and quiet for hours at a time. Camouflage practices were sometimes marginal.

Examples of US patrol activity

On Bataan in March 1942, the Japanese conducted raids with increasing frequency over several nights prior to conducting the main attack; these attempted to locate positions and take prisoners for interrogation. To counter this the Americans learned to launch their own raids and patrols, harassing the enemy and delaying their build-up, as well as locating troop concentrations to determine where the main attacks would be aimed.

After landing on Okinawa in April 1945 the US Army found the beach areas to be almost undefended, since the Japanese had withdrawn inland to prepared defenses. Enemy positions were so well camouflaged that they could not be detected from the air, nor were there man-made obstacles to indicate their location. Not knowing what to expect, US companies sent two-squad and full-platoon combat patrols forward accompanied by machine guns, bazookas and mortars, prepared to probe any enemy positions discovered to determine their extent. Gradually scores of such patrols fought their way into Japanese positions and then withdrew to report hard-won intelligence.

In the Hurtgen Forest in October 1944 the Germans had established extensive defences, which were difficult to locate in dense woodland shrouded in fog and persistent rain. The 29th Infantry Division employed squad-size patrols to scout along ridges and ravines; German

(continued on page 41)

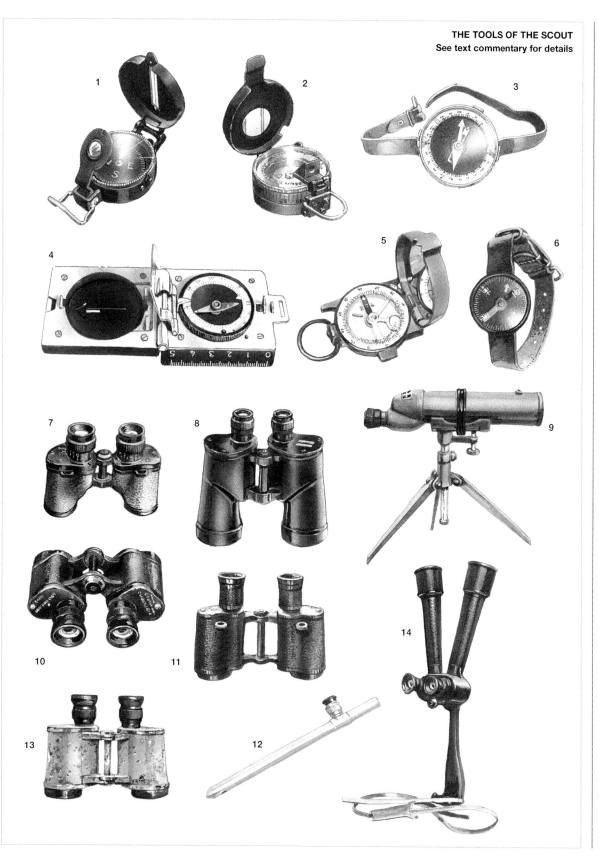

A

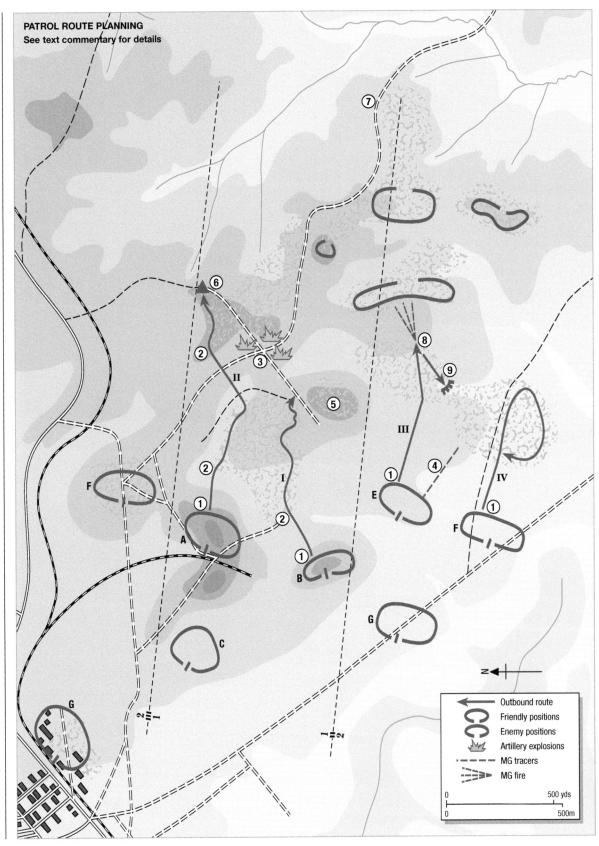

PATROL ROUTE PLANNING
See text commentary for details

Outbound route
Friendly positions
Enemy positions
Artillery explosions
MG tracers
MG fire

0   500 yds
0   500m

B

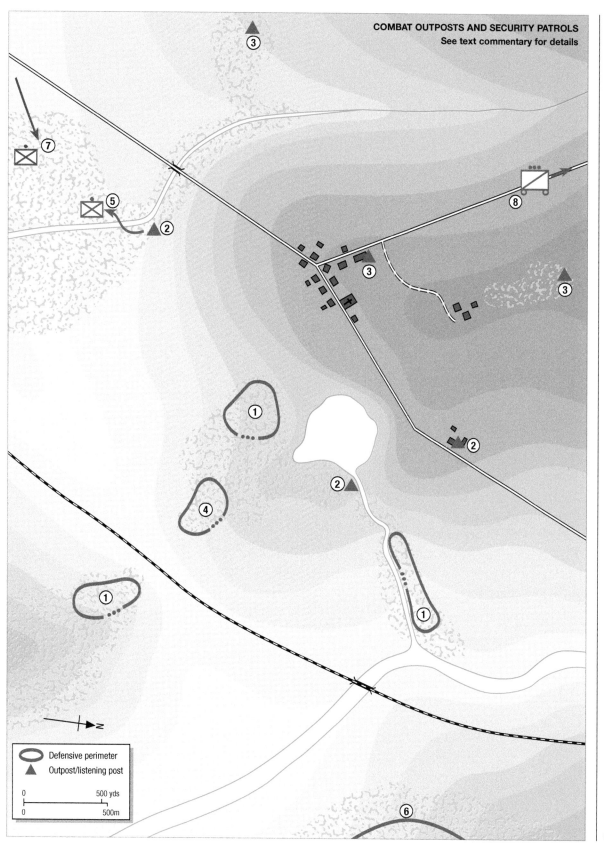

COMBAT OUTPOSTS AND SECURITY PATROLS
See text commentary for details

Defensive perimeter
Outpost/listening post

0   500 yds
0   500m

C

FOUR-WHEEL-DRIVE MOBILITY
See text commentary on page 41

D

BRITISH LIGHT ARMOURED RECONNAISSANCE
See text commentary for details

E

GERMAN RADFAHRTUPPEN
See text commentary for details

F

RED ARMY SCOUTS WITH FIREPOWER
See text commentary for details

G

In Normandy in summer 1944 a British observer uses a 20x telescope. For pure reconnaissance, the British favoured three-man patrols inserted one night, lying up to observe during the day and returning the following night. The close, overgrown terrain gave plenty of cover for daylight patrol movement; but on a crowded battlefield, divided up by small open fields and lanes, there was a high risk of coming under fire without warning. Fighting patrols not only stalked enemy snipers, but sometimes dropped off scout/snipers themselves – either to support the patrol's mission, or to remain behind and carry out their own task. (Crown copyright)

outposts prevented many from locating the main line of resistance, but eventually the persistent probes gained some information. Assaults were launched, but were badly hampered by the close and broken terrain, bad weather and scattered German positions. German units were often out of contact with each other, and prisoners did not know where adjacent units were located. This meant that repeated US patrolling was necessary before each new advance, to determine terrain conditions and enemy dispositions. Regimental I&R platoons often abandoned their jeeps and operated on foot, since the forest roads were covered by German fire.

GREAT BRITAIN

Britain had a long tradition of cavalry serving as scouts at all echelons. In 1939 each of the infantry divisions of the British Expeditionary Force sent to France had an integral battalion-size *mechanized divisional cavalry regiment*, with 28 light tanks and 44 armoured carriers; however, in April 1940, just before the Blitzkrieg was unleashed, these units were detached to form brigades in the GHQ reserve. The effectiveness of German divisional reconnaissance battalions in May/June 1940 was recognized; and after Dunkirk the Bartholomew Committee recommended the creation of dedicated reconnaissance battalions, with mechanized equipment and heavy firepower, to be attached initially to corps but later to each infantry division as availability allowed.

This Reconnaissance Corps was established in January 1941, by converting various existing units. The new units soon began using cavalry nomenclature, and this was retrospectively authorized in June 1942; divisional reconnaissance battalions, companies and platoons became *reconnaissance regiments*, squadrons and troops.[8] The regiment was equipped with armoured light reconnaissance cars (LRC) and tracked Universal ('Bren gun') carriers, light trucks and motorcycles; after experience in Tunisia and Sicily in spring-summer 1943 heavier armoured cars with turret guns were added. The regiment normally bore the same number as the parent division, e.g., 15th (Scottish) Recce Regt was assigned to the 15th (Scottish) Division. In January 1944 the Reconnaissance Corps was absorbed into the Royal Armoured Corps, and thereafter regimental designations were followed by 'RAC'.

British Reconnaissance Regiment (1942)
.303in rifles x 675, 9mm SMGs x 12, .303in LMGs x 126;.55in AT rifles x 48, 6pdr AT guns x 8, 2in mortars x 18, 3in mortars x 6 Light reconnaissance cars x 45, carriers x 67; motorcycles x 71, trucks/jeeps x 90
Personnel x 770

---

[8] See Elite 152, *The British Reconnaissance Corps in World War II*

October 1943, on the 5,500ft Shaggy Ridge in the Finisterre Mountains of New Guinea: two Australian 7th Div forward scouts photographed close to Japanese lines during the first patrol to get on to this strategic feature. Note that one has his 9mm Owen sub-machine gun modified to take two magazines; in the British and Commonwealth armies the SMG was the favoured weapon for the leaders and sometimes other members of patrols. After sustaining the first shock of the Japanese offensive in 1942, the Australians in New Guinea pursued aggressive patrolling tactics, often taking ambush positions on trails likely to be used by the Japanese. At night roving patrols would move quietly between friendly outposts to frustrate infiltrators, and for the same reason units covering rear areas would patrol or lay ambushes in the most difficult terrain, such as heavily overgrown ravines.

From 1942 the regiment was organized into an HQ squadron, which included AA, AT and mortar troops, and three recce squadrons. Aside from HQ vehicles, each squadron had two scout troops each with four LRCs (later 3x LRCs plus 2x armoured cars) and six carriers; and one assault troop with four eight-man rifle sections carried in light trucks, which provided integral infantry to secure objectives and carry out foot patrols. With a wide range of vehicles and heavy firepower, the regiment could perform all types of mission on any terrain; later some units even acquired US 75mm halftrack-mounted guns for heavy support. The types and numbers of vehicles varied in practice between units in different theatres; in the Far East, as with US units in the Pacific, most work was done with jeeps or on foot.

While initially intended for protective reconnaissance (screening and counter-reconnaissance), recce regiments were increasingly employed for reconnoitring in advance of a division, screening the flanks, securing gaps, and the same range of opportunist missions as the US Army divisional units. Recce units advanced under one of three protocols: 'move in green' – when enemy were unlikely to be encountered; 'in amber' – when contact was possible and speed was reduced; and 'in red' – when contact was likely, speed was greatly reduced, and close reconnaissance of possible enemy positions was conducted.

British armoured divisions underwent a bewildering series of reorganizations during the war; the reconnaissance asset evolved from none in 1940, to an *armoured car regiment* (58 x ACs) in 1942, to an *armoured reconnaissance regiment* (61 x medium plus 11x light tanks) in 1944. The 1st Airborne Division had a glider-borne squadron of MG-armed jeeps; 6th Abn Div had a small armoured recce regiment with mixed jeeps, scout cars, carriers, and two heavy troops each with 4x airportable light tanks.

Infantry brigades and battalions did not have a dedicated reconnaissance sub-unit, but the British battalion did have the advantage of a fourth rifle company, providing sufficient additional troops for patrols, outposts, flank security, etc. The infantry battalion also possessed a 53-man *carrier platoon* equipped with 13 Universal carriers, 12 motorcycles (four with side cars) and two light trucks. The carrier platoon, armed with LMGs and light AT weapons and mortars, was assigned a wide range of combat missions in both defence and offense to exploit its mobility and firepower. The fully-tracked carriers were valuable for intercommunication between exposed positions, and also for bringing up stores and supplies rather than burdening marching troops.

They were also valuable for reconnaissance, mainly being used for reconnoitring positions to be occupied by the battalion, flank reconnaissance to contact adjacent units, short-range daylight reconnaissance forward of the main defensive positions, and, during withdrawals, the reconnaissance of successive defensive positions. For these missions the carrier platoon could be reinforced with rifle sections, medium machine guns, mortars, AT guns and pioneers.

* * *

A British junior officer discussed what made for successful fighting and reconnaissance patrols in the US Army's August 1943 Intelligence Bulletin:

> The preparation of the patrols is done with detailed thoroughness. No fighting patrol is sent out until its leaders have spent at least a day watching the actual post they are after, and reconnoitring exact routes and so forth. If the leaders are not satisfied at the end of the day, they will postpone sending out the patrol, and will devote another day to the preliminaries. Some of our men are a little too inclined to think of a patrol at four or five [o'clock] in the afternoon, and send it out that same night. To be worth a damn, a fighting patrol must start off with an odds-on chance... not six-to-four or even money, but a good two-to-one bet. To make this possible, your information has got to be really good and up to date.
>
> As regards to composition of fighting patrols, there is a wide divergence of opinion. In this battalion we go on the principle of maximum firepower with minimum manpower, and our patrols have usually consisted of an officer, a noncom, and nine men – in other words, an assault group consisting of an officer, three [grenade]-throwers, and three Tommy gunners, and a support group of a noncom and three Bren gunners.
>
> The type of reconnaissance patrol which has produced the best result is the one composed of an officer or sergeant and two men, who go out at night, remain awake and observe all the next day, and return during the second night.'

Examples of British and Commonwealth patrol activity

In North Africa there were many instances of British and Australian night patrols infiltrating German lines and spending up to three hours collecting information – e.g. recording the locations of defensive positions, artillery positions, command posts and supply dumps. Other patrols ventured out into the desert to locate enemy minefields,

determining their width and density by feeling and probing – an excruciatingly slow and dangerous process. In the featureless desert night navigation was almost impossible; patrols would reconnoitre planned night routes during the day or in twilight, and place stakes mounting a tin with a torch inside – a small hole in the 'friendly' side of the can allowed the light to be seen for miles once darkness fell.

Desert reconnaissance patrols avoided contact and travelled as light as possible; only enough ammunition and grenades were carried – in cotton rifle bandoliers and pockets – to break contact, so web equipment could be left behind; knives were often carried for silent kills. The troops had to dress warmly in the desert night, sometimes in mechanics' overalls over sweaters; for the sake of quiet helmets were replaced by knit caps, and hobnailed boots by canvas-and-rubber or crepe-soled shoes, or socks were pulled over the boots.

The Australian garrison besieged in Tobruk in April–November 1941 were particularly aggressive patrollers and raiders. One eight-man raiding patrol had the mission of destroying a German MG nest and capturing prisoners. They infiltrated between outposts and forward positions, to circle well behind their objective. The patrol was not deterred by other positions which they slipped past at close range, nor by unaimed protective MG bursts; one enemy party working on a minefield were spotted, and avoided – these activities were recorded to be reported upon return. The raiders patiently worked their way behind the target MG nest until they were in position for it to be silhouetted against the rising moon. They initiated the attack with grenades, rushed the position, took a prisoner and wiped out the rest. Their return was equally slow, and even more dangerous now that the enemy were alerted; but in due time the patrol returned safely, with a valuable intelligence source and at the cost of two of its members slightly wounded.

In Malaya and Burma in 1941/42 the British and Commonwealth forces were shockingly outmanoeuvred by Japanese offensive tactics. Once stabilized on the India/Burma frontier they initiated a complete revision of infantry tactics for jungle fighting, with a strong emphasis on self-reliance by sub-units; there was a doctrine of aggressive patrolling, and infantry battalion HQs formed specialist platoons from rigorously selected officers and men. Infantry had to conduct extensive patrols owing to the restrictive terrain, scarcity of reconnaissance aircraft, and the Japanese propensity for finding trails not marked on maps. Patrols might be of any size from three men, through squad size, to platoon-strength fighting patrols. It was common for British patrols to operate up to 15 miles ahead of the forward units. In a sense, since effective fighting in jungle terrain demanded high levels of initiative from sub-units fighting in isolation, most infantry tactics had a strong input of patrolling disciplines.

In the Netherlands in autumn 1944, Lt Sydney Jarry of 4th Bn Somerset Light Infantry disagreed with the 'Battle School' prescription for a night fighting patrol of eight to 12 men, believing this number too difficult to control properly. Assigned to probe a suspected German platoon position in an orchard some three miles away, he preferred a six-man patrol: armed with a Colt pistol, he led out a two-man Bren LMG team with seven magazines, and three men with Sten SMGs and five magazines, all but the LMG team carrying four grenades each. Not spotted by a German security patrol which actually cut their file in two as they crossed a wire fence, they reached the objective. While infiltrating the position they were challenged and grenaded, but fought their way clear and returned safely. Jary (whose leadership of many patrols was recognized by the award of the Military Cross) considered that in quiet sectors fighting patrols were too often sent out for no good reason, believing this to be a hangover from the British World War I insistence on 'dominating No Man's Land'.

This Red Army mounted scout has three essential items: a sub-machine gun, binoculars, and a snow camouflage smock. When white camouflage clothing was not available, scouts would roll in the snow so that it would stick to their uniforms in patches; in extreme cold it would adhere for some time, and the mottling of olive drab and white actually provided better camouflage among vegetation than all-white clothing.

SOVIET UNION

Despite the massive size of the Red Army it possessed relatively small numbers of reconnaissance units. Numerous motorcycle battalions and regiments were raised in 1942–43, with most assigned to mechanized corps, and some survived to the war's end. Motorcycles were unusable in extreme cold, and some armoured car battalions were employed for reconnaissance – these had better mobility on frozen snow and better protected the crews from the wind. The USSR had a number of horsed cavalry formations; these mostly operated as unified offensive forces, but occasionally cavalry regiments or battalion-size squadrons were attached to other formations for reconnaissance. Ski rifle and aerosled battalions and regiments were formed in the winter, but these were mainly offensive rather than reconnaissance units. (Aerosleds – *aerosan* – were ski vehicles powered by aircraft engines, with a crew of two and mounting a machine gun.)

While man-pack radios were potentially invaluable to reconnaissance patrols, the 6-PK was typical of Soviet sets of the period: flimsily constructed, poorly designed for maintenance, and of mediocre performance. (Nik Cornish)

At the outbreak of war in 1941 the rifle division possessed a 328-man *reconnaissance battalion* (*razvédka batalón*), comprising single small motorized rifle, armoured car (10x BA-20), and tankette (16x T-37/T-38) companies, the armoured cars and amphibious tankettes being armed only with 7.62mm machine guns. These battalions were short-lived owing to huge losses, and in 1941/42 the reorganized divisions were assigned a small *reconnaissance company* (*razvédka kompániya*), which remained the divisional scout unit throughout the war.

Many Red Army organizations were smaller than Western units of similar designations; the reconnaissance company's authorized strength was 120, but by 1942 it had dropped to 103 men. It had an HQ, and three platoons each of three 12-man squads, each armed with an LMG, four SMGs and seven rifles. The platoon had three trucks and a four-man 50mm mortar crew; the small company HQ and three platoon HQs split up to ride in the squads' nine trucks. When company size was reduced they lost the mortars and some riflemen, but received more SMGs; the trucks were also withdrawn due to serious shortages, but the company were issued skis in winter, and some units used horses. Apart from its small size and light firepower, the main problem with the reconnaissance company, especially since it was a divisional asset, was that it had only one radio – a deficiency suffered by all Soviet units.

The infantry regiment had both a horsed and a foot reconnaissance platoon. The 22-man *mounted platoon* was intended for screening the flanks, with one of its two squads patrolling on either side of the marching regiment; the 49-man *foot platoon* scouted ahead with its four sections. In the defence, the foot platoon manned outposts and the mounted platoon patrolled forward as a screen. In 1942 the foot platoon lost one section. The 1943 regiment was authorized only an 11-man mounted and a 25-man foot 'platoon' – barely adequate for their missions. In many instances the horses were allocated elsewhere (or eaten), and the two platoons merged or disappeared altogether due to casualities.

* * *

The Soviets viewed the mission of reconnaissance units as purely information-collecting by stealth, avoiding contact with the enemy and leaving no trace of their presence. In contrast to combat patrols,

scouts did not normally 'fight for intelligence' – the term *razvédka* (reconnaissance) could also be translated as intelligence, scouting, or spying. This was one reason why they relied mostly on foot mobility, although this greatly hampered their range of action and their ability to report information. There were some units that used trucks to move sections within practical foot range of their objectives, and others that used horses, skis and snowshoes.

The 1942 *Combat Instructions of the Infantry of the Red Army* went into much detail regarding the rifle section conducting reconnaissance; these same techniques were employed by the reconnaissance company, which typically sent its squads out separately for independent missions. Squads were given a specific point or direction in which to reconnoitre forward of the security line – some 2km in daylight and 1km at night. Scouts would also be sent to the flanks if deemed necessary, up to 300m in daylight and 100m at night. Once in the area to be reconnoitred, the squad would establish successive observation posts to survey the area for signs of enemy activity. If necessary the squad leader, accompanied by one or more scouts, would physically reconnoitre the area while the bulk of the

German solo and combination motorcycles of a reconnaissance battalion line a road during a brief halt in Russia, summer 1941; the white 'G' painted on the headlight covers identifies Panzergruppe Guderian. The heavy armoured car is an SdKfz 231 Waffenwagen (weapons car) armed with a 2cm cannon and 7.92mm machine gun. (Courtesy Concord Publications)

squad remained in the OP to cover the scouts if they were engaged. The squad leader then designated the next OP, and the scouts proceeded to it with the rest of the squad following.

If they encountered an obstacle the scouts determined if it was covered by the enemy: if it was, they would attempt to find a way around; if it was not, they would try to move through it, marking a route. Separate buildings, small woods, large clumps of brush, ravines and other features that might hide the enemy would be searched. If individuals or small groups of enemy were encountered the patrol would attempt to capture them without firing. Areas that had been occupied by the enemy were thoroughly searched for anything of intelligence value.

The Soviet concept of reconnaissance-in-force (*razvédka boem*) employed troops in company strength, and frequently battalion or regimental strength. These were supported by concentrated artillery fire, and often by accompanying tanks. The main objective of such attacks was the taking of prisoners and sometimes the capture of important terrain features.

Outposts to prevent surprise attacks were established forward of the main line of resistance, up to 600m out in daylight and 200m at night.

Smaller satellite outposts might be established out to 200m from larger outposts. A large outpost was usually manned by a platoon or two squads, and a small outpost by a squad. This allowed the squad to operate in three shifts, posting two-man pickets on likely enemy approaches out to 100m in daylight and 50m at night. Pickets and small outposts were directed to halt individuals and send them to the rear with a guard; small enemy patrols were allowed to pass and be dealt with by larger outposts to the rear. If an enemy assault force was discovered the outpost commander would send a messenger to alert the larger outposts and parent unit. If the assault force appeared to be on a course that would discover the outpost, the latter was to open fire and withdraw. Upon returning from missions patrols would report any information of use to the outpost before they re-entered their lines and proceeded to the headquarters to report.

Red Army soldiers proved especially proficient in conducting reconnaissance in forests, swamps and mountains. While snow reduced their operational radius and speed, they used it to their benefit when skis and snowshoes were available – the Germans often lacked these, especially during their first Russian winter of 1941/42, to the detriment of their counter-reconnaissance patrols. Some Russians were familiar with skiing, but it was found that infantry units required 14 days of cross-country ski training, to include adequate physical conditioning. Specialist ski troops, including scouts, were given a two-month course, which included tactics and techniques.

The Soviets were adept at close-range ambushes on small groups such as German reconnaissance patrols, and at sneaking up to surprise isolated out-guards, in order to capture prisoners or intelligence information. Well camouflaged, they could lie in wait for hours until an opportunity presented itself. Squad-size night patrols might carry LMGs and 50mm mortars, while platoon-size patrols might add heavy MGs and AT rifles or even a 45mm AT gun.

The Soviets had learned a costly but useful lesson from the Finns in the Winter War of 1939–40: that the most valuable target for winter raiding patrols to destroy was the enemy's rolling field kitchens – being deprived of hot food and drink in extreme cold weather quickly reduces any enemy's effectiveness. When in defence, the Red Army also discovered the hard way that patrols were necessary not just to the front and flanks but to the rear as well, to ensure that enemy infiltrators or deep patrols had not cut their supply routes.

It should be added that the Soviets also made considerable use of civilians, especially children, for intelligence missions; children aged from 8 to 14 were given formal four-week courses to prepare them for such work. The Germans learned to round up lone civilians found in their sectors.

A German evaluation of Soviet patrolling techniques admits to their flexibility: 'On a stabilized front the Russian conducted his reconnaissance with patrols or reconnaissance-in-force. He was exceedingly adept at combat reconnaissance in offensive as well as defensive operations. He knew how to adapt his reconnaissance patrols to the terrain and how to employ them in great numbers. Seldom could any conclusion as to the intensions of the Russian enemy be drawn from his reconnaissance patrol activity.'

These Waffen-SS troops appear to be from 4.SS-Polizei Div; they are using a commandeered Russian boat to reconnoitre in a swamp – small boats were critical for operations in terrain such as the huge Pripet Marshes. The man partly off-camera to the right carries a Czechoslovak 7.92mm zv26 light machine gun, widely used by the Waffen-SS as the MG26(t). (Courtesy Concord Publications)

Examples of Soviet patrol activity

One encircled Red Army division was ordered to break out and fight its way back to Soviet lines. Dozens of daylight patrols were sent out to locate the weakest point in the encircling German lines. The forest was dense and there were only a few trails, no roads; the patrols were sent through the densest parts of the forest, reasoning that the Germans might have occupied such areas only weakly. Many patrols failed to return, but by nightfall a weak sector had been identified. The infantry regiments began to disengage and were directed to the weak sector, led by an assault battalion guided by the patrols which had discovered the opportunity; rearguards were left, to deceive the Germans into believing that the positions were still occupied. To reinforce the deception, platoon-size combat patrols were also sent out from all withdrawing regiments to aggressively probe other parts of the German lines, creating the impression that break-outs were being attempted. Many of these patrols perished, but some managed to break clear on their own.

In Stalingrad and other embattled cities the Russians employed two- and three-man teams of hand-picked scouts, to infiltrate the maze of shattered buildings and rubble and locate hidden gaps in German lines. They would mark the routes with strips of white cloth, and return to lead raiding and assault parties through German lines. These would attack command posts, mortar positions and supply dumps in the German rear, take prisoners, attack strongpoints from the rear, or establish their own strongpoints in the German rear to support frontal assaults.

GERMANY

Before the war Germany attached company-size squadrons from cavalry regiments (Kavallerie Regimenter) to infantry divisions when a reconnaissance capability was needed. There was also a bicyclist company attached to the AT battalion. At the beginning of the war, existing cavalry regiments were broken up and reassigned to infantry and mountain divisions. These regiments had two differently composed battalions: 1st Mounted Bn (I.Reiter Abteilung) had five horse-mounted squadrons, and 2nd Bicyclist Bn (II.Radfahrer Abteilung) had three bicycle squadrons plus AT, heavy weapons and signals squadrons under battalion control.

Each pre-war regiment provided the cadre for three to five *reconnaissance detachments* (Aufklärungs Abteilungen) for different infantry divisions; these were designated, e.g., Aufkl Abt der 7.Infanterie Division. Organization varied depending on the 'wave' in which the division was raised. First and second wave divisions mobilized at the beginning of the war had 623-man reconnaissance battalions composed of a small staff; a mounted squadron (Reiter Schwadron); a bicyclist squadron (Radfahrer Schwadron); and a heavy squadron (schwere Schwadron) with three 3.7cm AT guns, two 7.5cm infantry guns, and two or three light armoured scout cars. These latter were the MG-armed SdKfz 221 leicht Panzerspähwagen, the only AFVs in an infantry division; one was usually an SdKfz 222 Funkwagen (radio car). The third and fourth wave divisions raised from reservists after the war began had two bicyclist squadrons, and lacked the mounted squadron and armoured cars; and mountain divisions lacked the heavy squadron altogether.

The mounted squadron had three platoons each with a small 'platoon troop' or HQ, and three 12-man Gruppen (squads), each with one 7.92mm MG34. The bicyclist squadron was organized similarly, but the platoon troop had a 5cm mortar squad transported by two motorcycle/sidecar combinations; the squadron also had a heavy MG platoon with two tripod-mounted MG34s and 11 motorcycle combinations.

As the war progressed the battalion evolved. On the Eastern Front in 1942 many divisions were so badly mauled that their AT and reconnaissance battalions were consolidated into a single Panzerjäger und Aufklärungs Abteilung. In late 1942 they were redesignated *fast battalions* (schnelle Abteilungen); and in early 1943 the battalions were restructured. The nature of close combat now made horses impractical for aggressive reconnaissance; they were anyway in short supply, and the burden of caring for and feeding them was no longer worthwhile.

In October–November 1942, reconnaissance battalions were redesignated *bicyclist battalions* and numbered after their division in the usual manner – e.g. Radfahr Abteilung 7; the battalion now had two bicyclist squadrons and a heavy squadron. In March 1943 they were again redesignated as Aufklärungs Abteilungen, although some retained the previous designation. Between May and November 1943 many divisions redesignated their units yet again as the *divisional battalion* (Divisions Bataillon).

Their role changed drastically as the Germans went on the defensive on all fronts. There was now little need for an intelligence acquisition unit, but rather for a heavily armed, mobile combat unit as a division reserve and counter-attack force – on the extended frontages that they were assigned the often understrength division could not afford to keep one of their two-battalion regiments, or even a single battalion, in reserve. Beginning in July 1943 and through to November, all 'divisional' battalions and those still designated 'bicyclist' or 'reconnaissance' were redesignated yet again as *divisional fusilier battalions*.

German Reconnaissance Battalion (1941)
7.92mm rifles x 550, 9mm SMGs x 30, 7.92mm LMGs x 25; 7.92mm heavy MGs x 2, 3.7cm AT guns x 3, 5cm mortars x 3, 7.5cm infantry guns x 2 Armoured scout cars x 3, motorcycles x 50, trucks/cars x 49; horses x 260 Personnel x 623

When the new Type 1944 infantry division was fielded it was assigned one of these Divisions Füsilier Bataillonen, which was organized similarly to the rifle battalions of its infantry (now, for morale purposes, 'grenadier') regiments; the fusilier battalion had one heavy and three rifle companies, often completely equipped with bicycles.[9] Up to mid 1943 the reconnaissance units in their various guises had kept cavalry nomenclature, but this was abandoned once they became simply a divisional infantry reserve unit with no reconnaissance role.

Apart from the divisional units, infantry regiments had possessed since before the war a 35-man *mounted platoon* (Reiter Zug) as part of the headquarters. It consisted of a five-man HQ, a six-man train, and three eight-man squads (Gruppen) divided into two four-man 'marching details' (Abmärschen), the basic operating sub-unit of the cavalry. Each of the 29 mounted men was armed with a rifle and pistol – none had automatic weapons. The platoon conducted short range reconnaissance, screening, and served as couriers. During the invasion of Russia in 1941 they scouted far ahead, reconnoitring routes, locating the enemy and protecting resting foot troops. Scouting, ranging up to 80km a day, was especially important due to the inaccurate maps available. The horses were eventually replaced by bicycles, and in some instances by motorcycles.

The Waffen-SS basically paralleled the Army organizations, and used Army tactical manuals. Senior SS divisions possessed an SS-Aufklärungs Abteilung, although many of the later, lower-grade divisions had an SS-Füsilier Bataillon instead.

* * *

During the Russian winter snowshoes were provided to bicycle and mounted squadrons, and regimental mounted platoons might use them too. Some of these units, especially bicyclists, were also ski-trained. In North Africa motorcycles and Kübelwagen cars replaced horses and bicycles.

In the advance the reconnaissance battalion detachments operated up to 25–30km ahead of the division. They were to reconnoitre routes, prevent surprise attacks, gain superiority over enemy patrols and security forces, and locate the enemy; if confronted by superior forces they would yield and seek by-pass routes or more weakly defended sectors. The battalion's detachments might be reinforced by pioneer, AT and artillery sub-units. They also screened exposed flanks and gaps between advancing units. Whatever a patrol's mission, all were expected to conduct terrain reconnaissance (Geländeerkundung).

Horse-mounted troops had a range without resupply of 100km (62 miles), bicyclists 150km (93 miles) and motorized elements 250km (155 miles). Normal operating distance was a day's march ahead of the division, about 29km (18 miles), though motorized units usually operated an hour ahead, or about 40km (25 miles). The mounted squadron's three platoons, each augmented with a horse-mounted radio team, screened the division's flanks and spread out as far as 10km (6.2 miles). A bicycle platoon would move in advance of the division on its main route, while the rest of the squadron followed along with the heavy

---

[9] Grenadier regiments had enjoyed elite status in the old Imperial Army. On 15 October 1942 Hitler, in an effort to improve the morale of his worn-out infantry, redesignated all Infanterie Regimenter as Grenadier Regimenter; the individual Schütze (rifleman) was redesignated Grenadier.

A Waffen-SS interpreter conducts a field interrogation of a Soviet prisoner. One major mission of reconnaissance units was capturing prisoners in order to extract information of immediate tactical use; the Red Army slang for such a captive was a *yaziki* – 'tongue'. As German air reconnaissance was progressively limited by growing Allied air superiority, intelligence gained from prisoners became ever more important. (Nik Cornish)

squadron to overcome weak enemy resistance. The scout car platoon would reconnoitre sideroads along the main route. During normal operations the platoons would be out all day, returning at night to feed and rest the horses, but they might remain out all night if an early start was planned. When the division was in contact with the enemy they did little advance patrolling, being employed mainly to screen exposed flanks and gaps.

The infantry regiment's mounted platoon was mainly employed for reconnoitring ahead of the regiment and screening flanks. During the advance into Russia it was not uncommon for them to cover 70–80km (43–50 miles) in a day. The platoon had no radio so had to relay information back to headquarters by couriers – which meant that some men rode a lot further than that. In the defence, they screened the front to drive off enemy patrols, and served as couriers. There were instances when the platoon was reinforced with MG-armed rifle squads to undertake combat assignments; they might even serve as a regimental reserve, usually being augmented with machine guns.

With the later increased mechanization of reconnaissance units, light cars, scout cars, armoured cars and halftracks covered the front, with motorcycles used to cover gaps and 'thicken' the coverage. Scout car and armoured car combat reconnaissance (Gefechtsaufklärung) patrols typically comprised three vehicles, one of them equipped with radio; an artillery forward observer usually accompanied the patrol to call for emergency fires. Missions lasted one or two days, with clearly defined tasks and objectives. If enemy outposts were encountered, action was avoided unless they could be destroyed or driven off without diverting the patrol from its mission. Assault guns or tanks might be attached if strong resistance was expected. The AFVs of the patrol remained in sight of each other, but in open country they could be as much as 300 metres apart.

A pre-war Japanese patrol on exercises, with Mount Fuji in the background. Reconnaissance was part of the training, but was often neglected in practice, due to over-reliance on the strength of will (*seishin*), underestimation of the enemy, and the tendency to expect the enemy to do as the Japanese had anticipated. These men wear soft caps (with white identifying manoeuvre bands); these provided a less distinctive silhouette, and most are additionally adorned with foliage. At left, note the soldier with heavy expedient camouflage draped over his shoulders and pack. (Courtesy Akira Takizawa 'Taki')

When approaching obstacles the Germans assumed that they were under enemy observation, and the lead vehicle would reconnoitre-by-fire, shooting into possible positions. If fire was not returned men dismounted, attached tow cables, and pulled the obstacle down. If this was not possible pioneers breached it with demolitions. If the obstacle could not be breached or the terrain was impassable the patrol might dismount with machine guns and reconnoitre on foot, covered by the AFVs. When approaching a treeline one scout car might drive to the edge, halt to observe, and then rapidly drive off, enticing the enemy to fire if present.

* * *

A patrol or 'scout troop' (Spähtrupp) sent out by a rifle company typically consisted of an NCO and three or four men, with a 'getaway man' at the rear. They avoided contact and withdrew if fired on. Combat patrols (Gefechtsspähtruppen) were of at least squad strength, usually more, and well armed. Combat patrols of 15–20 men were organized into two groups each with a designated leader; one group would reconnoitre the objective while the other covered it. Pioneers might be attached to patrols to guide them through their own minefields and obstacles, or even to breach a passage for them. Combat patrols would also test the strength of enemy outposts; those found to be weak might be attacked, occupied, and reinforced.

'Patrols with special tasks' (Spähtruppen mit besonderen Aufgaben) were sent out for specific missions including destroying targets – either behind enemy lines or between the lines – with demolitions, ambushing convoys, attacking enemy patrols, laying mines on enemy convoy routes, or other harassing actions. The Germans sometimes registered mortars and artillery during the day on an enemy-occupied objective to be reconnoitred at night; after dark the objective would be shelled, and the waiting patrol would immediately move in for close reconnaissance while the enemy was still under cover or disorganized. Machine guns, mortars and artillery were co-ordinated to provide cover for the withdrawal of a detected patrol. Such fires might also harass a position adjacent to one being reconnoitred, to provide a diversion.

Soviet assessment of German patrol activity

A Soviet assessment of German reconnaissance was published in the US Army's September 1943 *Intelligence Bulletin,* and provides firsthand insight on the subject. It is also provides some information on Soviet counter-reconnaissance:

> The Germans place great emphasis on reconnaissance. Dozens of orders and memoranda issued to German Army units include reminders that land reconnaissance must be conducted by all branches, regardless of whether or not this type of work is their primary responsibility.
>
> During periods of inactivity on the front, German reconnaissance attempts to learn: (a) location and extent of our defensive lines; (b) location and composition of our strongpoints; (c) differences between our day and night dispositions; (d) location of our obstacles and minefields; (e) movements and new positions of our units.
>
> German reconnaissance tries to report accurately and in detail the dispositions of our troops, heavy artillery, headquarters and reserves. Regarding all changes in our units as significant, the enemy attempts to discover these changes and to draw conclusions which can be put to use. This reconnaissance is carried out by observers, listening sentries, patrols, or battle (reconnaissance-in-force).
>
> Special attention is given to the reports of the listening sentries. Under cover of darkness, these men crawl as close to our lines as possible and try to plot and fix the location of various sounds – especially to gain information about our tanks, reserves, the movement of our patrols, the location of new artillery positions, and areas in which digging is in progress. Although the listening sentries can sometimes discover important data, we are repeatedly able to deceive them by means of ruses. Since the listening reports are checked in the daytime by German visual observation, we are obliged to deceive the visual observers, as well, for the sake of consistency. For example, if we imitate tank sounds at night for the benefit of German scouts in a certain locality, the next day we must see to it that there is some sort of camouflage in the same place.
>
> Reconnaissance by a combat patrol – usually a platoon – is most often done at night. These patrols, armed with grenades and machine pistols, generally operate without artillery support. They try to reach positions on the flanks without attracting attention, and then suddenly attack a previously assigned objective for the purpose of capturing a [prisoner for interrogation]. In general, the objectives are those which have been discovered by lookouts and listening scouts. After capturing a number of outposts, the Germans send details of two and three men into our rear areas. Our wide-awake unit commanders often take advantage of these tactics for the purpose of counter-reconnaissance.
>
> If the Germans are unable to locate our outposts and flanks or believe them to be well hidden, reconnaissance by a patrol is preceded by artillery and mortar fire. Under such circumstances the raiding party is divided into attacking and supporting groups. As a rule, one or two small groups make a frontal advance, while the

remainder attack the designated objective from the flanks. Two or three days before this type of operation, the Germans place ranging fire on the objective and nearby positions. After this preparatory fire, the Germans do not fire again in this area until they are ready to attack. However, during daylight it is not difficult to detect the movements of small groups of soldiers who are being instructed in the methods to be used for the attack and fire support. It is also fairly easy to detect a group of officers on a reconnoitring mission. When the Germans are thoroughly prepared, they launch a night attack. If Russian units detect the approaching groups and open fire on them, the Germans signal for the previously prepared artillery and mortar fire.

Reconnaissance-in-force is the most ambitious of all German reconnaissance missions. As a rule, it is directed against a well-fortified position, and precedes an offensive. Before such a reconnaissance, small groups, like those described above, will have tried to define the boundaries of the main objective. The unit which is to perform such a reconnaissance may vary in size from a company to a battalion with artillery support. If the Germans expect to encounter unusually well-fortified positions with prepared obstacles, a unit consisting of engineers, heavy artillery and tanks is integrated into the reconnaissance party.

The Germans try to conduct a reconnaissance-in-force with all the speed they can achieve. If their first attempt is unsuccessful, they often repeat an attack, sometimes immediately after the first failure. Such an attack generally occurs during the second half of the night or at daybreak. During the daylight hours the objective is placed under intensified observation.

JAPAN

Detailed reconnaissance was a matter of doctrine, but it was often neglected in favour of impatient aggressiveness. This was a serious flaw, as the Japanese strove to attack from unexpected directions with surprise and speed; they also preferred night attacks, for which good intelligence was even more essential. Before conducting a night attack elements of the attacking units would probe the enemy positions to locate machine guns and other positions, but the Americans quickly learned to hold their fire, calling for mortar fire and throwing grenades to hamper the Japanese patrols, and keeping on the lookout for infiltrators. The blind attacking rush frequently led to costly Japanese failure.

Doctrine called for extensive reconnaissance during the approach march or meeting engagement. A co-ordinated attack was preferable, but the Japanese would not hesitate to commit units piecemeal, immediately upon arrival in the battle area and without reconnaissance. It was common for hastily attacking, unco-ordinated units to be cut off, destroyed or repulsed; they often attacked into strongly held positions or in the wrong sector.

Infantry divisions were provided with a 950-man *cavalry regiment* (*kihei rentai*) with an HQ and train, one machine-gun company and three rifle/sabre companies (some had only two companies). Even though this unit had almost 1,000 men it was organized as a battalion. The company

Japanese Cavalry Regiment
6.5/7.7mm rifles/carbines x 500,
6.5/7.7mm LMGs x 28;
6.5/7.7mm HMGs x 18, 2cm AT rifles x 4, 3.7cm AT guns x 2,
5cm grenade-dischargers x 18.
Trucks – very few; horses x 1,100.
Personnel x 950.

Japanese Reconnaissance Regiment
6.5/7.7mm rifles/carbines x 260,
6.5/7.7mm LMGs x 28;
6.5/7.7mm HMGs x 4,
3.7cm/4.7cm AT guns x 4, 5cm grenade-dischargers x 16.
Armoured cars/tankettes x 7,
Trucks x 61; horses x 188.
Personnel x 730.

A drawing of a Japanese patrol in the desolate mountains of China; a scout peers over the edge of a steep slope that the patrol will have to descend. While it was awkward in close country, the Japanese and Soviets generally patrolled with bayonets fixed, prepared for instant close combat and the silent kill. (Courtesy Akira Takizawa 'Taki')

had three platoons each armed with three LMGs and two 5cm grenade-dischargers ('knee mortars'), plus a two-gun HMG platoon. The machine gun company had two platoons each with two HMGs and two 2cm AT rifles, plus a platoon with two 3.7cm AT guns, and an ammunition platoon. The regiment had some 1,100 horses – which served well in China, but were withdrawn for deployments in South-East Asia and the Pacific islands; there these units operated on foot. Some units in SE Asia at least partly equipped rifle/sabre companies with bicycles.

Most infantry divisions were assigned a 730-man *reconnaissance regiment* (*sobaku rentai*), also a cavalry branch unit; these gradually replaced the cavalry regiments. The unit consisted of a 130-man HQ and train, a mounted company, two truck-borne companies, a tankette or armoured car company, and a truck transport company. The 130-man horse-mounted company had four 30-man platoons; the 160-man truck-borne company had two 50-man rifle platoons, a 24-man machine gun platoon with two HMGs, and a 24-man AT platoon with two 3.7cm guns. The tankette or armoured car company had seven AFVs – but many units, even in China, lacked this company. The 100-man truck transport company had two platoons – at least on paper – with one to transport each truck-borne rifle company.

In practice, especially in the Pacific, the reconnaissance regiment was much smaller and less heavily equipped than this. The 'mounted' company might have bicycles, but more frequently operated on foot – as did the two truck-borne companies, since the trucks were left on rear island bases as logistics transport. The truck-borne companies typically lacked their two AT guns, and tankette/armoured car companies (if they existed) were not deployed. As a result of these reductions the reconnaissance regiment for Pacific operations basically consisted of three rifle companies armed similarly to infantry companies, and fielded between 500 and 600 men. Divisions possessing cavalry regiments tailored them similarly, and they too were reduced in strength in the Pacific; some may have organized with four smaller companies.

Since Japan was fighting on the defensive after 1942, reconnaissance became secondary. Reconnaissance and cavalry regiments were deployed differently by different commanders depending on the size,

A Japanese patrol, heavily camouflaged, wades down a stream in South-East Asia; if an enemy aircraft approaches they can simply hug the bank. While resulting in uncomfortably wet trousers and boots, following a stream was much faster and less tiring than following faint animal trails through the jungle.

terrain, and tactical situation of the island on which they fought. They might conduct some reconnaissance, especially early in an operation; might be employed as a reserve, or be assigned to beach defence in other parts of the island after the main US landing; might secure an airfield or a second line of defence, or be employed as just another infantry battalion in the line.

Some divisions lacked a reconnaissance or cavalry regiment altogether, but might have a *tankette company* (*keisokosha chutai*) in lieu. Triangular infantry divisions usually possessed a small infantry group headquarters to control the three infantry regiments, and this HQ usually had a tankette company for reconnaissance. It should be noted that very few tankettes were employed against US forces in the Pacific – a handful on Namur Island and some on Luzon. The 80- to 120-man companies had ten to 17 x Type 92 (1932) or Type 94 (1934) tankettes armed with a single 7.7mm machine gun and crewed by two men. While considered ineffective in conventional warfare, tankettes had earned a useful reputation in China for reconnaissance and line-of-communications security, and Japan produced them in large numbers.

There were no organic reconnaissance elements assigned to infantry regiments or battalions. Tactical radios were simply not available to reconnaissance units and patrols, who were forced to rely on runners or waited until their return and debriefing to report information.

* * *

The 1938 *Military Operation Field Service Regulations* (*Sakusen Yomurei*) provided basic guidance for the conduct of patrols:

A man who is in charge of reconnaissance must be bold, cool, ardent, and responsible. The numbers, formation and equipment of the patrol should be decided according to the purpose and mission of the patrol, the movement of enemy, terrain, and other conditions. The selection of members, especially that of leader, is very important.

The patrol on foot must act in secret. At night, it can approach close to the enemy so it can accomplish its mission. When sending a patrol, the objective of the reconnaissance and the time of return should be clearly set. The time should be sufficient to accomplish the mission. When sending a patrol at night a single objective should be assigned. If possible, a guide light should be set to indicate the direction to the objective [meaning unclear: perhaps a light was set up on a known point in the friendly front line as a navigation reference point?] Soundproofing of equipments is necessary.

To maintain observation on the enemy for a long time, it is better to lie hidden in one place. It is necessary for the patrol to fully understand the general circumstances and purpose of reconnaissance and plan the route and method of the reconnaissance in advance. The main method of scouting is observation, but if an enemy patrol or small unit is encountered act aggressively as far as the mission allows. The usual method is for the patrol to move from one observation point to another point. The leader sometimes advances alone or with a few scouts, leaving behind the remainder. When taking a rest halt, search for a suitable place in advance; take care not to relax observation and alertness during the rest. In hostile areas never use the same place [more than once] for rest halts and bivouacs, and do not halt for a long time in or around villages. At night, frequently change the patrol's location. For communications, use radio and simple ciphers [but see above re: shortage of radios]. To identify one another at night use a challenge and password.

Patrolling on the larger islands in the Solomons and New Guinea required special skills owing to the dense jungles and broken ground; chance contacts with Allied patrols were common. Camouflage was critical, and Japanese soldiers learned to excel at it – though they had had no previous jungle experience or special training in similar terrain.

Examples of Japanese patrol activity
Patrols were frequently employed to harass the enemy and entice him into revealing his positions at night. In the Philippines in spring 1942 small patrols constantly employed individuals and small groups to fire from unexpected positions, sniping, deliberately making noise and fleetingly revealing individuals in unexpected places, and throwing firecrackers to create confusion. These tactics were only effective against green troops.

Small groups would infiltrate through gaps in American lines and around the flanks, remaining in hiding during the day until sufficiently strengthened by other groups on subsequent nights to launch attacks on targets in the rear or to support the main frontal attack.

British troops in Malaya in early 1942 reported that Japanese who infiltrated their flanks and rear would shout 'Withdraw!' in good English when the frontal attack began; this occasionally worked. The main assault groups talked and sang loudly during their approach to distract the defenders and cover the movement of the infiltration groups. In the Netherlands East Indies, infiltrating Japanese would learn the names of Australian and British officers by eavesdropping at night. Later they would call out their names to get a response and locate them, or order them to withdraw.

In 1942 in Burma the British – and on Borneo the Dutch – reported that patrols would expose some men to draw fire, and then infiltrate to knock out the detected MG positions. They would infiltrate through barbed wire, located by patrols during the day, quietly cutting the wire and attacking armed with knives; other Japanese would rap bamboo sticks to distract the defenders while the infiltration was in progress.

In Malaya the Japanese would induce local natives to move ahead of their advancing forces posing as refugees, who would then report British locations. On New Britain in 1944–45 the Japanese defending their Rabaul redoubt used sympathetic natives as an outer screen to warn of approaching Australian patrols; the same was done on New Guinea.

In Malaya a four-man Japanese patrol armed with LMGs infiltrated through British lines and killed 26 men in a brigade command post. In the Philippines, two- and three-man patrols with a single LMG would infiltrate, and their random attacks in the rear inflicted a psychological impact. Infiltrators who located an Allied MG or mortar position would pinpoint these for Japanese mortars by the converging tracer fire of two LMGs.

On Pacific islands it was found that Japanese patrols often covered surprisingly long distances by crawling on their stomachs at a snail-like pace, to get into observation positions or infiltrate lines. Time after time the patience of the Japanese soldier was demonstrated during infiltration and waiting in ambush; they were known to wait for hours to ambush the enemy, sometimes up to their necks in irrigation canals beside roads.

The Japanese preferred small patrols, but in dense vegetation, because of the greater danger of ambush, these tended to be larger. On Guadalcanal in 1942 a US Marine patrol ambushed a 25-man Japanese patrol, killing 18 of them; the patrol's size allowed some to fight their way out and return to Japanese lines with the intelligence they had collected.

FURTHER READING

Buchner, Alex, *The German Infantry Handbook 1939–1945: Organization, Uniforms, Weapons, Equipment, Operations* (West Chester, PA; Schiffer Publishing, 1991)

Daugherty, Leo J. III, *Fighting Techniques of a Japanese Infantryman, 1941–1945: Training, Techniques, and Weapons* (St Paul, MN; MBI Publishing, 2002)

Forty, George, *British Army Handbook 1939–1945* (Stroud, UK; Sutton Publishing, 2002)

Forty, George, *Japanese Army Handbook 1939–1945* (Stroud, UK; Sutton Publishing, 1999)

Jary, Sydney, *18 Platoon* (Carshalton Beeches, UK; Sydney Jary Ltd, 1987)

Tsouras, Peter G. (ed), *Fighting in Hell: The German Ordeal on the Eastern Front* (London; Greenhill Books, 1995). Compilation of reprinted US Army studies written by former German officers.

Zaloga, Steven J. & Ness, Leland S., *Red Army Handbook 1939–1945* (Stroud, UK; Sutton Publishing, 1999)

Handbook on the British Army with Supplement, TM 30–410, 13 September 1942
Handbook on USSR Military Forces, TM 30–430, 1 March 1946
Handbook on German Military Forces, TM-E 30–451, 1 March 1945
Handbook on Japanese Military Forces, TM-E 30–480, 1 October 1944

PLATE COMMENTARIES

A: THE TOOLS OF THE SCOUT

Besides weapons and communications equipment reconnaissance troops required few special tools, but two were critical: compasses and binoculars. The scout needed the compass, a relatively simple direction-finding device, to navigate to the objective, locate it, and accurately report it. Two basic techniques are 'intersection' and 'resection'. The location of a point can be determined by first plotting the azimuth to it from one known point on the map, e.g. a road junction; and then moving to a second known point, e.g. a barn, and plotting the azimuth to the enemy position from there. The azimuth lines are drawn on the map, and where they intersect is the enemy position's location; its grid co-ordinates on the map can then be reported or artillery fire called in. Resection enables a scout uncertain of where he is to locate himself by plotting the azimuth from his position to an object, e.g. a hilltop, that can be identified on the map. He then plots a second azimuth to another identifiable point, e.g. a church steeple. He draws these two lines on the map, and where they intersect is his location.

Infantry compasses were of two basic types: the more usual hand-held one carried in a pouch, and one mounted on a strap like a wristwatch. Compasses were graduated in three systems of angular measurement: in degrees (360° to the full circle); in mils (6,400 to the full circle, so 1 degree = 17.777 mils); or in Russian mils (6,000 mils to the full circle, so 1 degree = 16.666 Russian mils.) Wrist compasses were suitable only for approximating azimuth, but most hand-held compasses had a flip-up sighting device for more precise direction-finding.

Al: US lensatic compass, graduated in degrees for routine navigation and mils for adjusting artillery fire.
A2: British Mk III prismatic marching compass, graduated only in degrees.
A3: Soviet wrist *kompas*, graduated in Russian mils.
A4: German *Marschkompass*, graduated in mils. All nationalities dropped the final zero off degree numbers and the final two zeros off mil numbers.
A5: Japanese prismatic compass (*rashin*) graduated in mils.
A6: Japanese wrist compass of very simple design, with unnumbered mil graduations.
A7: US Army 6x30 M13 binoculars.
A8: US Navy 7x50 Mk 1 Mod 2 binoculars, used by US Marine Corps.
A9: US 20x M49 observation telescope on M15 tripod. This 14⅛in long scope was a light, handy and powerful tool for observers.
A10: British 5x No.2 Mk II binoculars.

Reconnaissance patrols did not just collect information by scouting; they might establish a temporary observation post behind enemy lines to detect activity. Here a German mountain trooper observes with 6x30 Sf14Z Scherenfernrohr ('scissors binoculars') – also called, for obvious reasons, Eselohren ('donkey's ears'). Note the lens tubes to prevent reflections from revealing the OP. In the US forces this type of equipment was termed a BC (battery commander's) scope. (Courtesy Concord Publications)

A11: Soviet 6x B-1 *binokl'*.
A12: Soviet 4x TR scout periscope (*razvedchik periscop*). This 14½in long tube allowed the scout to peer over walls or crests, and if held horizontally, around trees and corners.
A13: German 6x30 *Einheits-Doppelfernrohr*.
A14: Japanese 10x periscope binoculars, with chest brace and adjustable strap.

B: PATROL ROUTE PLANNING

Patrols were not simply sent out to wander about aimlessly; they were assigned a mission, specific tasks, a route and an objective. They had to establish a known location for departure – a reference point from which to plot their route. A route was assigned through an area where they might encounter or avoid enemy activity, depending upon their mission. It was necessary for higher headquarters to know the patrol's route in order to provide fire support, and to prevent friendly fire or other patrols running into it. The return route (not shown on the plate) was equally important: if at all possible it would be different from the outward route, but would bring the patrol back to the departure point (**1**), to prevent confusion and mistaken identity. Checkpoints (**2**) might be designated en route to aid navigation; and for the same reason artillery or mortar fire (**3**) or machine gun tracers (**4**) might be brought down on designated terrain features at pre-planned times.

The armoured cars used by divisional reconnaissance units were cramped – as demonstrated here by an American M8; all the crew's packs and bedrolls had to be stowed on the outside of the vehicle. The four-man crew consisted of the commander/loader and gunner in the turret and the driver and co-driver in the front hull. The co-driver had few specific duties beyond periodically relieving a tired driver, and when a unit took casualties this post was often left vacant.

Here we show patrol activity in adjacent regimental sectors. Patrol I from Company B of a battalion is reconnoitring a hill (**5**) to determine if it is occupied by the enemy; they will observe it from several positions. Patrol II from Co A is establishing a short-term OP (**6**) to direct artillery fire on an enemy supply route (**7**). Patrol III from Co E first conducts a diversion for Patrol I by placing MG fire from (**8**) on a known enemy position at a scheduled time; and then establishes an ambush (**9**) in hopes of surprising an enemy patrol. Patrol IV from Co F is a local security patrol conducted in an area where enemy patrols have previously been detected.

C: COMBAT OUTPOSTS AND SECURITY PATROLS

All armies practiced essentially the same 'layered' techniques for outposts and security while in defence or when halted – e.g. for the night – during an advance. A defensive line was established, with each unit in the line providing its own security – here, a company has established platoon positions (**1**, **1**, **1**). Each platoon put a small outpost or listening post, usually of two to four men, a short distance out – seldom more than 100 yards – to cover terrain offering a concealed approach (**2**, **2**, **2**). The company would deploy one to three outguards (**3**, **3**, **3**) further out, usually within 1,000 yards but sometimes as far as 1½ miles; these would cover roads entering the unit's sector. Usually these men were provided by a squad from the company's support platoon (**4**), and might be reinforced with machine guns, light anti-tank guns or infantry AT weapons. Squad-size security patrols (**5**) from the forward platoons or perhaps from the battalion's reserve company (**6**) would be sent out beyond the security line, not only to report the enemy's approach but also to keep enemy patrols at bay (**7**). Larger fighting patrols from the reserve company or the regiment's/brigade's reserve battalion, up to platoon strength, would move further afield. The regimental/brigade reconnaissance element and sub-units of the divisional reconnaissance unit (**8**) would be deployed even further out, because of their mobility.

D: FOUR-WHEEL-DRIVE MOBILITY

The ¼-ton four-wheel-drive 'jeep' was renowned for its mobility, and was widely used by all US, British, Commonwealth and many other Allied services. Here, armour plate has been added to one of the jeeps of the I&R platoon of the HQ company of a US Army infantry regiment – the 115th, from the 29th Inf Div – probing forward in the Rhineland in February 1945. Both jeeps have had the windshield removed, and both are fitted with vertical angle-iron 'anti-decapitator' bars on the front bumper – these were more for deflecting downed telephone and power lines than to cut wires intentionally strung across roads. Both jeeps are armed with the .30cal M1919A4 machine gun, on the M48 dashboard mount in the lead vehicle and on the M31 pedestal mount in the nearer jeep. Suspecting an enemy presence on their up-slope flank, the crews have partly dismounted to adopt firing positions.

E: BRITISH LIGHT ARMOURED RECONNAISSANCE

Few light armoured fighting vehicles were employed by reconnaissance units below divisional level, but the British infantry battalion included a carrier platoon assigned to the battalion support company. Equipped with 13 Universal tracked carriers – one in platoon HQ, and three in each of four sections (squads) – this versatile platoon was employed in wide range of roles including mobile outposts, flank security and reconnaissance. The low profile and compact size of the 4½-ton vehicle were valuable, though its 4mm-10mm armour offered protection only from small arms fire and shell fragments, and it had no overhead protection from grenades, airbursts, or fire from above as it drove up or down slopes. However, if engaged the platoon had considerable firepower: 13x .303in Bren LMGs, 4x AT weapons (until 1943 the .55in Boys AT rifle, later the PIAT projector), and 4x 2in mortars. The crews – one NCO and two privates in addition to the driver/mechanic – also carried rifles, by 1944 the Lee Enfield No.4 Mk I.

Here, somewhere in northern France after the Normandy break-out in August 1944, the sergeant commanding a section of three carriers from 3rd Inf Div is being briefed by the platoon sergeant, who is armed with a 9mm Sten SMG and rides a Norton WD16H – one of the three motorcycles assigned to platoon HQ, along with one carrier and two 15cwt trucks. The trackguard markings identify the division, and the junior battalion – white '57' (1st South Lancashire Regt), of the division's senior brigade – red background (8th Inf Bde). Each of the other two carriers is commanded by a corporal.

F: GERMAN *RADFAHRTRUPPEN*

The standard German Fahrrad (bicycle – 'Rad' for short) was the Truppenfahrrad 38; various other civilian makes were also employed, as was the Austrian Waffenrad made by Waffenschmied. Many bicycles were finished in black rather than Army dark field grey. Standard features included hand brakes, headlamp with blackout cover, bell ringer, air pump, a tool and spares kit in a rectangular tin box, and a rear cargo rack for the rider's personal equipment; a machine gun tripod, 5cm mortar or ammunition boxes could also be packed on this.

Here, in Russia during a summertime advance, a patrol has come under fire from the treeline on the edge of a village and takes cover to return fire. The leader of the Gruppe (squad) fires a signal round vertically from a 2.6cm Kampfpistole – this 'battle pistol' resembled a flare pistol but with a heavier, rifled barrel for alternative types of ammunition. The orange smoke round will burst overhead in two seconds, marking his location for friendly aircraft; he has already marked the enemy position with a white smoke round. A Truppenfahrrad 38 and a Waffenrad (with tool box) have been discarded against the fence as the riflemen scatter under cover.

German coloured smoke signalling

In North Africa the Germans and Italians used a standard coloured smoke marking system to convey simple instructions and information to their own aircraft:

Colour(s)	Meaning
Orange	Axis troops here (or, distress signal)
Orange-red	We are isolated/the enemy is behind us
Orange-green	Repeat your attack
Green	Increase range of action as we are advancing/attacking/making contact
Red	Enemy is attacking/infiltrating/penetrating
Red-green	Enemy is attacking/encircling on our right
Red-white	Enemy is attacking/encircling on our left
Violet	Enemy tanks ahead
Violet-red	Enemy tanks in our rear
Violet-green	Enemy tanks to our right
Violet-white	Enemy tanks to our left
Violet-orange	Friendly tanks going into action

In other theatres the Germans used red smoke as a standard ground-to-ground warning to 'beware of enemy AT weapons', and blue or violet to warn 'enemy tanks present'. Orange always indicated German troop locations, and white marked Allied targets.

G: RED ARMY SCOUTS WITH FIREPOWER

While the German Army suffered badly from lack of suitable clothing and equipment during their first winter in Russia, 1941/42, and from shortages during subsequent winters, the Red Army took advantage of their relative familiarity with the conditions. While most troops were not ski-trained some reconnaissance units fielded ski sub-units, hastily trained after the first snows fell. Fleece caps, padded uniforms, sheepskin coats and (when not skiing) large felt boots all offered protection from the elements, and white over-garments gave concealment; this patrol, moving outafter a brief halt during a patrol in winter 1942/43, have the later issue two-piece suits. It was not uncommon for infantry reconnaissance patrols to carry a preponderance of sub-machine guns (here the PPSh-41) and to be liberally supplied with grenades; but patrols were also issued with heavier weapons – while taught to avoid contact with superior forces, if they were engaged they were expected to break

A sketch depicting an Australian infantry patrol – of two-squad or platoon size – receiving its mission briefing and drawing ammunition. Experienced front-line troops tended to develop standard procedures for patrols which speeded up their deployment: orders were streamlined and kept simple, and routine actions, movement formations, signal instructions, weapons and ammunition allocation did not have to be specified for each mission.

through by 'vigorous action'. When conducting a reconnaissance in force, besides its standard one or two 7.62mm DP light machine guns the rifle squad was often augmented with a 50mm mortar ('mine thrower', here the RM-41), and/or a 14.5mm PTRD-41 anti-tank rifle.

H: JAPANESE RECONNAISSANCE BY STEALTH

Most reconnaissance was conducted at night, when advancing Allied forces had halted; here we show a four-man team working their way forwards in the Solomons or New Guinea. They have got within small-arms range, and advance at a painfully slow crawl, making good use of dense vegetation and terrain irregularities to approach as close as possible to a defensive line of American foxholes. The sound of their movement may have been masked by artillery harassing fire or aircraft overflights. If the Americans' noise-and camouflage discipline is poor, they will merely observe silently before withdrawing to report back. If not, they may open fire, throw grenades or shout in attempts to trick the defenders into firing or otherwise giving away their positions.

Movement through jungle terrain required a great deal of patience and determination; the humidity of the climate, thorny vegetation, and such jungle creatures as stinging ants, centipedes and snakes made crawling very uncomfortable. Faces and hands were camouflaged with charcoal or mud; local reeds, grasses, leaves or other vegetable fibres were used to fashion camouflage capes resembling the traditional rice-straw rain cape of the Japanese peasant.

German patrols were known for their ability to infiltrate through enemy lines even in daylight, by using ditches, shallow gullies, low folds in the ground and scattered vegetation.

INDEX

Printed and bound by CPI Group (UK) Ltd, Croydon, CR0 4YY

12/04/2022

03119725-0008